D0414087

H. G. WELLS

H. G. WELLS

A COLLECTION OF CRITICAL ESSAYS

Edited by

Bernard Bergonzi

Prentice-Hall, Inc. *Englewood Cliffs, N.J.*

A SPECTRUM BOOK

Library of Congress Cataloging in Publication Data
MAIN ENTRY UNDER TITLE:

H. G. Wells : a collection of critical essays.

(Twentieth century views) (A Spectrum Book)
Bibliography: p.
CONTENTS: Bergonzi, B.—Introduction.   West, A.
H. G. Wells.   Weeks, R. P.—Disentanglement as a
theme in H. G. Wells's fiction.   [etc.]
    1. Wells, Herbert George, 1866–1946—Criticism
and interpretation—Addresses, essays, lectures.
I. Bergonzi, Bernard.
PR5777.H2   823'.9'12   75-34492
ISBN 0-13-950048-0
ISBN 0-13-950030-8 pbk.

10 9 8 7 6 5 4 3 2 1

PRENTICE-HALL INTERNATIONAL, INC. (*London*)
PRENTICE-HALL OF AUSTRALIA PTY. LIMITED (*Sydney*)
PRENTICE-HALL OF CANADA, LTD. (*Toronto*)
PRENTICE-HALL OF INDIA PRIVATE LIMITED (*New Delhi*)
PRENTICE-HALL OF JAPAN, INC. (*Tokyo*)
PRENTICE-HALL OF SOUTH-EAST ASIA PRIVATE LIMITED (*Singapore*)

Contents

Acknowledgments

Acknowledgment is gratefully made to the Estate of H. G. Wells and to William Heinemann Ltd. for permission to reprint excerpts from *The Time Machine* and *The Island of Dr. Moreau.*

Acknowledgment is gratefully made to the Estate of H. G. Wells for permission to reprint excerpts from the following: *When the Sleeper Wakes, Kipps, The Food of the Gods, The Undying Fire, Tono-Bungay, The First Men in the Moon, Love and Mr. Lewisham, The Wheels of Chance, The War in the Air, The History of Mr. Polly, First and Last Things, In the Days of the Comet,* "Zoological Retrogression," and *The Refinement of Humanity.*

Acknowledgment is gratefully made to Harcourt Brace Jovanovich, Inc., and Faber and Faber Ltd. for permission to reprint two short excerpts from "The Waste Land," from *Collected Poems 1909–1962* by T. S. Eliot.

The author acknowledges with thanks the timely advice he received from Patrick Parrinder whilst this book was in preparation.

Introduction

by Bernard Bergonzi

H. G. Wells lived through the Second World War and died in 1946, shortly before his eightieth birthday. He was by then the author of well over a hundred books and in the last of them, *Mind at the End of Its Tether*, published just after the war, he seemed to reject humanity in anger and despair: "The end of everything we call life is close at hand and cannot be evaded."

Wells may not quite have believed this; he was always an inconsistent, impulsive thinker and the writings of his old age are particularly incoherent. Indeed, the last thing he published, an article in a left-wing London paper in July, 1946, attacking the monarchy, ends up with quite a cheerful injunction to continue the struggle for the universal welfare of mankind. Yet a mood of despair, if not totally dominant, increasingly came to possess Wells during his final years. He had begun life as a Victorian and had lived long enough to see the triumph of barbarism and the destruction of his hopes for a rational, scientific future for mankind. This point is developed by Anthony West in the influential essay that opens the present collection. Mr. West argues that Wells's late despair was a return to the scepticism and pessimism that inspired his scientific romances of the 1890s, and that the characteristically "Wellsian" vision of his middle years—the confident projection of an improved humanity steadily progressing by means of science and social planning towards a Utopian future—was an attempt to conceal and forget what Wells knew in his heart about human limitations. Something like this view has been accepted by those recent critics—including the present writer—who are more interested in Wells as an imaginative writer than as a commentator or prophet. It is true, certainly, that Wells was known to the reading public as a progressive and optimistic visionary for the best part of forty years, and writers on Wells who sympathize with the Utopian vision argue that his plans and projections for the future of humanity were all an exercise in the conditional mode: *if* men would unite, act rationally, make the best possible use of science, plan for a better society, then a glowing future of unlimited possibilities was assured. But in the end, as Auschwitz and Dresden and Hiroshima witnessed, mankind not only failed to live up to Wells's hopes and expectations, but adapted scientific resources and large-scale social engineering to new and unimagined extremities of death and devastation.

It would be a mistake to underestimate the power, and even the permanent effects, of the positive Wellsian vision of the early decades of this century. During the First World War Wells was one of the planners of the League of Nations, which can be seen as a forerunner of the United Nations and the various world organizations of our own day. Indeed, Wells was accustomed to thinking in global terms long before his contemporaries, and he liked using the word *world* in the titles of his books, from *The War of the Worlds* in 1898 to *Guide to the New World* in 1941. In other ways, too, Wells's influence may have been much greater than we suspect. His early scientific romances captured the imagination of the English-speaking world and very possibly influenced the subsequent development of technology; not, indeed, by visible cause-and-effect, but by inspiring scientists to realize certain fascinating, if remote, possibilities. Thus, the First Men in the Moon of 1969 might never have stood where they did if it had not been for Wells's fictional anticipation of the event some seventy years before. Yet space travel seems at best an ambiguous good, as well as being very expensive; a world more and more conscious of the shortage of global resources will reject Wells's assumption that the riches of nature are limitless and should be exploited fully for the good of humanity. It might, indeed, be possible to present, by careful selection from his voluminous and often self-contradictory writings, the image of an ecologically responsible Wells. Yet the case for Wells as an analyst of the human condition and a guide to a better future, if it is still to be made, will need strong and convincing arguments: it can no longer be taken for granted among large segments of liberal opinion, as it once was.

Nevertheless, Wells remains remarkably interesting as man and writer, if no longer a reliable guide and teacher, and has been the subject of several recent biographical studies. Wells began his literary career in the 1890s, and the course of his later development, whether in fiction or in discursive writing, was fixed in a certain *fin de siècle* mould. As we move, with apocalyptic fears and imaginings, towards the end of our own century—and the end of a millennium too—the culture of the last *fin de siècle* exerts a steady fascination, even to the extent of inviting re-enactment. Wells first made a name for himself in 1895 with *The Time Machine*, a short novel of great literary distinction; it remains a marvellously imaginative story, full of mythic implications, and, I believe, Wells's finest piece of fiction. It presents a vivid picture of humanity in full decline and even, in the end, of the extinction of life on the great globe itself. The final years of the nineteenth century were intensely formative for Wells. They were, on the one hand, a period of *fin de siècle* anxieties about the future, to which Wells gave colorful form in the local or global catastrophes of *The War of the Worlds* and *The Time Machine*. On the other hand, the nineties were also a time of eager aspirations, when the growth of socialism and popular education and scientific progress seemed to promise a new and transformed future for the mass of humanity. Wells was peculiarly a product of that age of transitions and new frontiers. He grew up in Bromley, Kent, and, over the years, saw it change from a country town to a London commuter suburb, as he recalled in 1911 in the autobiographical opening chapters of *The New Machiavelli*. His family was poor but shabby-genteel, with the father making a precarious living by selling china and playing professional cricket and the mother acting as a housekeeper to the gentry. Wells exhibited a marked kind of social loneliness, fearing the working class and envying the solidly established middle classes. He was the first "scholarship boy" among English intellectuals, and he is almost unique among imaginative writers in having had a scientific rather than a literary or classical training. Indeed, it was the tension between the scientific education Wells acquired during the 1880s at the Royal College of Science, where the great Thomas Huxley was briefly one of his teachers, and a fertile imagination much given to images of collapse and destruction that produced the most memorable effects of his science fiction.

Before the turn of the century Wells's visions of the future were apocalyptic, even terrifying, and he found the prospect of disturbing his readers very satisfying. In *The War of the Worlds* he shows the comfortable bourgeois society of West Surrey, where he was then living, subjected to every kind of horror and destruction from an army of Martian invaders. While writing it Wells would bicycle around the neighboring countryside looking for suitable places for the Martians to ravage. After 1900 Wells's interest in the future became much more positive, and in *A Modern Utopia* (1905) he wrote his first famous Utopian fantasy, which tried to project a better world, conditional perhaps, but described with ingenuity and enthusiasm. (Though as the sceptical Chesterton remarked, the ingenuity was all directed to showing how the secondary problems of distribution and administration would be solved, once the really intractable question of changing human nature had been disposed of.) There were, admittedly, still projections of a grim, destructive future, as in *The War in the Air* (1908); but Wells's interest in the future became more systematic and more positive and was realized in a series of Utopian scenarios, culminating in his attempt to write a long and detailed history of the future in *The Shape of Things to Come* (1933), which is now principally remembered as the source of a classic science-fiction film.

Wells's perennial fascination with the future did not prevent him from writing *The Outline of History*, in which he turns to the past and boldly attempts to trace the global development of the whole of humanity. It was a great success as a work of popular education, though Wells's attitude to the values that have sustained Western civilization is often briskly philistine. He was not very interested in the past for its own sake, preferring to see it as a morass of muddle and confusion and ignorance from which a struggling humanity had to extricate itself. Yet, in a special sense, Wells's imagination was haunted by his own recent past. On the negative side, there were the struggles to escape from a narrow and constricting environment, to achieve a career and, in the end, success as a writer. But there were positive aspects too, as, for example, when Wells affectionately recalls rural England in the last decades of the nineteenth century, like the Kentish fields and streams, still unaffected by urban sprawl, that he had explored as a boy at Bromley. A little further afield there was the kind of countryside that might be gently traversed by bicycle, as does the hero of his first fictional comedy, *The Wheels of Chance* (1896). Wells, like Mr. Hoopdriver, was a keen cyclist as a young man, and this fact gives his vision of England a certain historical location. For a few years in the nineties the bicycle and cheap railway excursions gave lower-class English people free access to a countryside that was still quiet and unspoiled and seemingly rooted in traditional ways. It is this aspect of rural England that Wells returns to in many of his novels, whether in the delightful evocation of Sussex village life in the opening chapters of *The Invisible Man*, or the surprisingly respectful description of Blades-over, the great country house in *Tono-Bungay* (based on Up Park, where his mother had once been housekeeper) or the pastoral retreat of the Potwell Inn, where Mr. Polly finds an ultimate haven. By the turn of the century the peace of the countryside was disturbed by the new rich man's toy of the motorcar, as it made its noisy, dirty, and often dangerous progress along rural roads that had previously known no more advanced machine than the bicycle. The advent of the motorcar provides a new motif in Edwardian fiction, whether in Kenneth Grahame's *Wind in the Willows* or E. M. Forster's *Howards End*. With his conscious mind Wells was in favor of motorcars, as of every other form of scientific progress; but in the deeper reaches of his imagination he preserved his allegiance to the quieter, less aggressively exploited England that he had known in his youth and early manhood. For all his iconoclastic impatience, Wells's radicalism contained a strong streak of nostalgia, which directed his gaze back to a harmonious but vanished rural order; the same tendency is noticeable in later English writers of left-wing conviction, such as George Orwell and Raymond Williams.

Wells continued to be a novelist until the end of his life; that is to say, many of the books that he wrote can be classified as fiction. He did not lose all the basic skills in writing that had once made him so widely admired as a novelist, and his later fiction is often readable and amusing, as Wells displays his iconoclastic humor. But these books are carelessly written and self-imitative in a way that tries to recapture the success of his Edwardian fiction. Moreover, they are written not simply to tell a tale but to point a moral; from about 1911 onwards Wells came to believe that fiction should be didactic, should raise and ventilate all the large questions of the day, and should help humanity in its constant struggle to a better life. It was a plausible ideal but it did not help the fiction to endure; when the issues died, so did the novels that enacted them. As examples one need only refer to the series of novels that Wells published between 1911 and 1914, all dealing with the problems of love and marriage and fidelity: *The New Machiavelli, Marriage, The Passionate Friends*, and *The Wife of Sir Isaac Harman*. Only the first of them retains much interest; partly for its quasiautobiographical element, and partly for its reflection of Edwardian political battles, not for its insights into the difficulties of marriage. Although, as a young man in the 1890s, Wells had taken the art of fiction very seriously, both as a critic and a practising writer, by 1914 he had ceased to regard it as an art at all. "I had rather be called a journalist than an artist, that is the essence of it," he wrote in 1915 at the climax of his celebrated quarrel with Henry James about the nature of the novel. But it is only art that endures.

Even in the field of ideas Wells continued to draw throughout his long life on the intellectual matrix of the *fin de siècle*, and the complications of twentieth-century history increasingly left him behind. He was in essence a millenarian thinker, always looking for the overthrow of the established order and the coming reign of the Saints, whom he projected in his Utopian writings as a powerful and dedicated ruling elite. These rulers, who owe something to the Nietzschean notion of the Superman, which was fashionable in Wells's formative years, were first depicted as the Samurai of *A Modern Utopia* and subsequently recur in various versions, culminating in the wise, aloof airmen of *The Shape of Things to Come*. We have seen enough of ruling elites in action to be suspicious of such ideals and are not likely to share Wells's assumption about the basic wisdom of technocrats and administrators. The one book of Wells's later years that still remains vigorously alive is his *Experiment in Autobiography* (1934), which is fascinating as a narrative, as an essay in deliberate self-revelation, and as an exposition of some of the major forces at work in the intellectual and cultural history of England around the turn of the century.

But for the most part Wells's later work can be let go, particularly if our main interest is in imaginative literature. That is why the present collection of essays is largely devoted to the first fifteen years of Wells's literary career, the period between 1895 and 1910, when he published most of the fiction that has endured, whether in his scientific romances, or in comic-cum-realistic novels. These, indeed, are the works that have continued in public favor and have been widely read and often reprinted: on the one hand, *The Time Machine*, *The War of the Worlds*, *The Invisible Man*, and the fantastic short stories of the eighteen-nineties; on the other, *Kipps* and *Tono-Bungay* and *The History of Mr. Polly* of the Edwardian years. It can hardly be accidental that these were the years when Wells still took the art of fiction seriously and considered it proper to tell a story for its own sake. It is perhaps a reflection on the intractable nature of the human imagination, and one which would have angered the later Wells, that his writings are most truly literature when their vision of the future is apocalyptic rather than Utopian, and when they are more concerned with human beings in their lonely and struggling individuality than with large schemes for collective betterment.

All the essays in this collection were published since 1946, the year when Wells died, and most of them were written in the past fifteen years. It has taken time for Wells to fall into perspective, so that what is valuable can be distinguished from the rest of his bulky *oeuvre*. During Wells's life most of his critics, whether enthusiastic or hostile, were too much concerned with his ideas to be able to see his work as literature. Nevertheless, some significant essays were published, and they are listed in the bibliography to this book, notably those by G. K. Chesterton, D. H. Lawrence, Christopher Caudwell, and George Orwell. Though the contributors to this volume do not ignore either Wells's ideas or the events of his life, they have a common aim of preserving, or perhaps saving, him for literature.

H. G. Wells

by Anthony West

I find it difficult to write dispassionately of H. G. Wells. One of my earliest memories of him, too early for me to date, is of the occasion on which I first discovered the physical aspect of death. It was at a time when I had a treasure box, a small cigarette tin I believe, with a hinged lid. In it I kept some of the old-fashioned glass marbles, a button with a coat-of-arms upon it, and a few things of that kind which had taken my fancy. To these I one day added a few heads of snapdragon. I hoped that I would find them there in their bright prettiness whenever I wanted to look at them. But when I opened the box again after several days had gone by it held corruption and green moulds, and I screamed with dismay. I do not remember all the details of what followed, but I remember taking refuge from H. G.'s incomprehension under a gate-legged table, and I remember his lifting the edge of the table-cloth to peer in at me where I crouched, still screaming in grief and fear, and muttering "I just don't understand you."

It was a phrase he repeated, and with the same bewilderment, to me during his last illness. He was sitting with a light rug over his knees on a chair which had been placed where he could catch the sun on the grassed-in balcony at the back of his house in Hanover Terrace. We were sharing silences rather than talking. He was already extremely weak, and he husbanded his energies through long drowsy periods in which he seemed almost comatose, surfacing, so to speak, only occasionally when he wished to give his full attention to something or somebody. I would go to see him, in the hope of catching his interest and drawing him up to the surface. I wanted to drive out of his mind an impression—I do not care, even now, to think how he had been given it—that I had been "got hold of" by a pro-Nazi conspiracy somehow entrenched in the British Broadcasting Corporation which was then employing me in its News division. These conspirators were, he had been told, blackmailing me in some way and forcing me into some mysteriously discreditable line of conduct for an arcane ulterior purpose, the nature of which I have never been able to discover. This nightmare cobweb of misunderstanding had fallen between myself and my father in the first stages of the V-1 attack on London; it remained upon our faces through all the time the attack lasted, through the stranger time of V-2, until the war receded into the Pacific and left London in shocked and stunned silence. At first my father seemed too ill to be bothered with the necessary explanations. Then he made a partial recovery and I was able to hope. I sat with him often, when I was not on duty in the newsroom at the B.B.C., longing for the moment when he would open his mind to me. But the occasion never came, and at last I became aware that it never would. Sitting beside him one day, at once in the closest proximity to him and utterly remote from him, and, thinking him asleep, I fell into a passion of misery and buried my face in my hands. How long this spasm of pain lasted I don't know, but when its intensity slackened I suddenly became conscious that I was being watched. I looked up to find his eyes fixed upon me with all the clarity of his fully-conscious mind behind them. We stared at each other for an instant before he said, once again, "I just don't understand you." Then the light left his face. He had, as it were, turned himself off, and had relapsed into his dozing state on the frontier between sleep and death. The last chance of communication had gone, and there was never to be another. Rather more than a year later I chartered a boat named the *Deirdre* owned by a Captain Miller of Poole in Dorset, my half-brother came down from London bringing with him H. G.'s ashes, and we went out to scatter them on the sea at a point on a line between Alum Bay on the Isle of Wight and St. Alban's Head on the mainland. As we returned I found myself surprised at the extent of my bitterness. That I should have preferred my father to realize that I had been going through a sufficiently banal marital crisis, rather than to believe that I was falling into the hands of blackmailers who had been using me as a tool for treasonable purposes, was easy enough to understand. But that I should feel so violently about the matter when he was no longer in a position to believe anything at all shocked me, as it still does.

It will be realized why in those circumstances a self-protective device told me that Wells's mind was clouded by illness at a much earlier stage than it probably was to any significant extent. For some years after his death I reacted angrily to the criticisms of the quality of his thought which made so much of the extreme pessimism of his last writings and utterances. These were, and still are, being represented as an abandonment of a superficial optimism in the face of those realities of which his coming death was a part. The suggestion is made that they were some kind of final admission that he had been wrong about the nature of things for the greater part of his life. I felt at one time that this was a wilful exploitation of the auto-intoxication of a very sick man who no longer enjoyed full command of himself. But since sifting my recollections of his talk, and doing a great deal of preparatory work on his biography, I incline to another view. I cannot now agree that his final phase of scolding and complaining at human folly represented any essential change in his views at all. What happened as his powers declined from 1940 onwards was that he reverted to his original profoundly-felt beliefs about the realities of the human situation. He was by nature a pessimist, and he was doing violence to his intuitions and his rational perceptions alike when he asserted in his middle period that mankind could make a better world for itself by an effort of will.

This contention may seem grotesque to those who have a picture of him firmly entrenched in their minds as a kindly, avuncular figure promising men a birthday with lavish presents every week if the scientists were only given control of society. Last year Dr. Bronowski took time off from his duties as Director of the Coal Research Establishment to tell Section L of the British Association:

> H. G. Wells used to write stories in which tall, elegant engineers administered with perfect justice a society in which other people had nothing to do but be happy: the Houyhnhnms administering

the Yahoos. Wells used to think this a very fine world; but it was only 1984. . . .

This represents the received view. Mr. St. John Ervine in his life of Shaw asserts that Wells believed that infinite social progress was inevitable unless there were some global catastrophe; and George Orwell attributed his final despair to a belated realization that science was just as effective on the side of evil as on the side of good. And only the other day Mr. Geoffrey Barraclough, Professor Arnold Toynbee's successor in the Stevenson Research Chair of International History in London, was telling us that the evolutionary conception of society found its supreme expression in Wells' *Outline of History*. According to him this postulates that

> the development of intelligence is the work of 'natural selection,' and that inexorable laws of natural selection will result in the replacement of the present imperfect society by one in which a finer humanity will inhabit a more perfect world.

The diffuseness and looseness of much of Wells' writing, and the tone of a great deal of his occasional journalism, lends itself to this distortion of his basic ideas. But the fact remains that the body of work which bears his name contradicts these assumptions about his views, and the reader who undertakes to examine all of his writing scrupulously is in for a number of surprises. Wells received a scientific education and he never fell into the fallacy of confusing the Darwinian conception of evolution with the idea of progress. The idea of progress depends fundamentally on a picture of the universe in which mind is increasingly valuable, and which is also increasingly orderly. Wells' first serious piece of writing was a paper called "The Rediscovery of the Unique" of which he remained proud throughout his career. Though it does not reach a standard which would be acceptable to professional philosophers and logicians, it restates with clarity and force the idea which Hobbes put forward in *Leviathan* (I, iv) when he says that there is "nothing in the World Universal but Names, for the things named are every one of them Individual and Singular."

This is the foundation stone of the mechanistic view according to which the whole world is "nothing but a mere heap of dust, fortuitously agitated" and the universe a similar aggregation. It is impossible to believe in progress if you believe in a universe in which mind figures as a local accident, and which by its nature cannot support any permanent moral order or indeed any permanent thing.

That Wells was deeply committed to this view is evident from his first novel, *The Time Machine*, which has its climactic scene at a point some thirty million years in the future. The planet has ceased to revolve. It no longer supports human life, and it is evident that the time is rapidly approaching when it will no longer support life at all. A cosmic catastrophe is impending which will finally obliterate the material context in which such concepts as mind, consciousness, and value can possess any meaning. The possibility of such a situation is irreconcilable with the idea of progress, and Wells states his disbelief in it in this book without ambiguity. The questions which the Time Traveller asks himself on the first phase of his journey into the future are interesting, and revealing:

> What might not have happened to men? What if cruelty had grown to be a common passion? What if in this interval the race had lost its manliness, and had developed into something inhuman, unsympathetic, and overwhelmingly powerful? I might seem some old-world savage animal, only the more dreadful and disgusting for our common likeness—a foul creature to be incontinently slain.

What is implicit in these questions is the idea that an evolutionary trend that would make a man a more intellectual animal might also make him a much less humane one. This not only questions the idea of progress, but also suggests that virtue is not innate in the intellect as Victorian moralists were inclined to believe. I stress this point because it seems to me to be an important one if one wants to understand Wells' thinking. The conventional picture then was, and still to a considerable extent is, of a conflict between mind and man's animal nature, with the virtues seated in the intellect and the defects in the instincts and the animal behaviour patterns. Wells suggests that morals and ethics have their basis in man's behaviour as a social animal. That is to say that disinterested behaviour develops from a hunting animal's practice of bringing food back to its lair for its mate and its young; and that humanitarianism, and the sympathies that make life endurable, develop from the animal habit of snuggling in a huggermugger, as puppies or kittens do, for warmth. The intellect on the other hand is amoral and ultimately recognizes the single value of efficiency, so that a continuation of the line of development that had made man a reasoning animal might ultimately make him more callous, indifferent, and cruel, and not more moral. This nagging fear of the liberated intellect as something inhumane was to play an important part in Wells' later work, but he raised in it *The Time Machine* only to drop it in favour of an explicit statement about natural selection. The premise is that the nineteenth century layered class society constituted an artificial environment to which man was adapting himself. The donnée for the purpose of *The Time Machine* was that it was going to endure; so the Time Traveller finds, in the year A.D. 802701 that adaptation has divided the human race into two distinct subspecies. The descendants of the old ruling and propertied classes live above ground and fear the dark, those of the workers and managers subterraneously in fear of the light. Both are hopelessly degenerate, and neither considers the Time Traveller to be an old-world savage, because neither group is capable of sufficient sustained thought to frame so elaborate a concept. It is with something of a shock that one finds that what has brought about their debasement is precisely the complete success of mankind in establishing a technological society and world order of the kind to which Wells is supposed to have given his unqualified endorsement. At some point during the eight hundred thousand year interval men completely mastered their environment and solved all the social problems. When they were comfortable they stopped thinking, and then degenerated along the lines of their own inherent weaknesses.

One of the difficulties of writing about Wells is that his mind was undisciplined, and that on any given point he can be found either to contradict himself, or to appear to do so. *The Time Machine* was immediately followed by *The Island of Dr. Moreau*, which Wells discussed much later, in the twenties, as if he had accepted a dualistic picture of human nature while he was writing it: "Humanity is but animal rough-hewn to a reasonable shape and in perpetual internal conflict between instinct and injunction."

This would give innate virtue a refuge in the intellect, and would allow for optimism as a possibility. But what happens in *The Island of Dr. Moreau* is a disaster, the liberated intellect in the person of a Darwinian humanitarian arrives on the island and disintegrates its theocratic moral order by making an appeal to reason which assumes that Dr. Moreau's victims are moral creatures with better natures. When they are set free from the Hobbesian régime of terror under which they have been living it is revealed that they are, beneath Dr. Moreau's scar tissue, brutes interested only in the satisfaction of their appetites. So far as a conflict between instinct and injunction goes, it is no contest; order and law are imposed on the brutish inhabitants of the island by an exterior force, and as soon as that is removed the system collapses. What the book in fact expresses is a profound mistrust of human nature, and a doubt about the intellect's ability to contain it. There is even a doubt about the intellect as a possible containing force, since its role in the story is a purely destructive one.

The Island of Dr. Moreau relates closely to two other stories, a short novel and a short story, which deal with the same theme of the liberated intellect as a destructive element. *The Invisible Man* is a parable about the amoral aspects of the scientific outlook, and invisibility figures in it as a symbol of intellectual isolation. "The Country of the Blind" is a much more mature version of the same parable, in which the symbolic situation of the sighted man in the community of the blind is even more harrowing. In both stories men are cut off from normal human feeling and corrupted by the sense that their special knowledge gives them a right to power over the unenlightened. They both end by running amok in the same lonely terror which overtakes the visitor to Dr. Moreau's Island. The theme is carried further in *The War of the Worlds* and in *The First Men in the Moon*. The Martians, like the ruling class on the moon, are brain cases with the merest of vestigial bodies, symbols of the intellect triumphant over the animal. The point that technological mastery has given the Martians a sense that they are free from moral responsibility is obscured by the surface action in *The War of the Worlds*. Most readers do not see beyond the fact that the Martians arrive, and treat Europeans as Europeans had been treating native populations and animals in the hey-day of colonialism, to the deeper argument. But there is no possibility of misunderstanding the description of lunar society which appears towards the end of *The First Men in the Moon*. The unfettered intellect rules, and respect for efficiency stands in the place of morality. What has come into being is the worst kind of slave state. It has reduced most of its members to simple automata. Many of them are actually deformed physically to fit them more precisely for specific social functions. When the labourers of various types are not required they are laid aside in induced coma until they are needed. Wells' scientist, Cavor, reports on this society with naïve approval, so that there can be no doubt about what he is getting at. The clear implication is that a further extension of human intellectual powers in the post-renaissance direction of abstract rational thinking will lead to the growth of cruel and inhuman planned societies which will be utterly indifferent to human values and individual happiness. Human sympathies will be stifled, and endless cruelties perpetrated in the name of an abstract common good, because logical analysis finds that human sympathies have no basis in the sort of reality that it can recognize. The scientific apparatus for examining reality is hostile to values in so far as it shows that any system of values is purely arbitrary. In the end, what Wells is saying in *The First Men in the Moon*, is that the basis of operations which Huxley recommended in his famous Romanes lecture, and which he had himself adopted and stated in the concluding paragraphs of *The Time Machine*, is not viable. Because if a mechanistic view of the universe is constructed by the right hand the left will inevitably loose its grip on any ethical system it may have decided to grasp.

It may seem that this is reading something into *The First Men in the Moon* which is not there, but Wells went out of his way to state it in a mundane context in *When the Sleeper Wakes*. Many people recall this novel of 1899 as a description of the triumph of gadgetry with its descriptions of flying machines, television, public address systems, and air-conditioned roofed-in cities. It stands as the optimistic and naïvely uncritical forerunner of Aldous Huxley's *Brave New World*, and Orwell's *1984*. In fact Wells' society of 3002 includes many of the worst features of both these later constructions. It "features" a deliberately debased and systematically misinformed proletariat, constant surveillance and thought control, and an amoral brutality; and these things are described as evils. The difference between Wells' horrors and those described by Huxley and Orwell reside mainly in points of detail. Wells was writing before the two great wars and the dictatorships had made the State as dangerous an engine as it now seems. For Wells the enemy was monopoly capitalism as it presented itself in the form of the great corporations. But his business State is just as monstrous as the police State of Orwell's imagination, and is perhaps worse in that it does not bother to persecute individuals as individuals, but simply treats people in terms of social categories and utility. Wells' equivalent of Big Brother, Ostrog, the head of the super-corporation's governing body says:

> "I can imagine how this great world of ours seems to a Victorian Englishman. You regret all the old forms of representative government . . . the voting councils and Parliaments and all that eighteenth-century tomfoolery. You feel moved against our pleasure cities. I might have thought of that—had I not been busy. But you will learn better . . . the pleasure cities are the excretory organs of the State, attractive places that year after year draw together all that is weak and vicious, all that is lascivious and lazy, all the easy roguery of the world, to a graceful destruction. They go there, they have their time, they die childless, and mankind is the better. . . . And you would emancipate the silly brainless workers that we have enslaved, and try to make their lives easy and pleasant again. Just as they have sunk to what they are fit for . . . I know these ideas; in my boyhood I read your Shelley and dreamt of liberty. There is no liberty save wisdom and self-control. Liberty is within, not without . . . suppose that these swarming yelping fools in blue [the proles wear blue uniforms] got the upper hand of us, what then? They will only fall to other masters. So long as there are sheep Nature will insist on beasts of prey. It would mean but a few hundred years' delay. The coming of the aristocrat is fatal and assured. The end will be the Overman—for all the mad protests of humanity. Let them revolt, let them win and kill me and my like. Others will arise—other masters. The end will be the same."

From this viewpoint in 1899 Wells was able to see that the growth of a technological society would throw up régimes much worse than those of such simple-minded tyrants as Napoleon III. Ostrog is more like Hitler than anything which had then been seen, he was probably conceived as a criticism of Carlyle's hero worship, while the society he presides over is a criticism of the structural aspects of Plato's *Republic*.

I have dwelt on these early books of Wells' because they seem to me to show how foreign to his thought the ideas that either evolution or technical development would inevitably produce a moral order, or even a better order, were. I think, too, that the view of human nature taken in these early books accounts for the flaw in the later ones which now makes them seem ill-considered and confused. These are forced in so far as they say things which Wells wishes to believe, and in which he, ultimately, does not believe. What he ultimately does not believe in is the ability of the human animal to live up to its ideals. *The Time Machine*, *The Island of Dr. Moreau*, and *When the Sleeper Wakes*, all state this idea quite bluntly. In mid-career Wells stopped saying this and adopted the progressive line, stating a body of ideas which can be called Wellsian.

These can be summarized roughly as follows. Education and the liberal tradition have produced a disinterested group of men of good will capable of taking hold of the drift of modern life and of giving it coherent direction. Cheap paper and mechanized printing together with the prosperity and leisure produced by industrialization have made universal education a practical possibility. An educated community (as distinct from a merely literate one) would be able to establish rational relationships with other communities. Improved communications would bring these educated communities into increasingly close contact with each other and a world community would develop. A sense of kinship would grow up among all men, and instead of squandering their creative potential in pointless and destructive wars they would learn to settle their differences by negotiation and agreement. A world order would take shape in which racial, regional, and national frictions would have no place. Men would work happily together to bring each other a fair share of the world's abundant wealth. There are no logical objections to this as a plausible future course of development for human society if the romantic view of human nature is once accepted, and man is taken to be a creature of infinite possibility. If man is such a creature, it is then just a matter of adopting this rational aim and

making a great collective effort to secure it. Wells wished to
proceed, and to persuade other people to proceed, on this basis.
But he knew that in the long run all human effort was futile and
that man was base. The world was Dr. Moreau's Island and the
men of goodwill were building on sand with obdurate material
which by its essence excluded any possibility of success. Wells'
"progressive" writing represents an attempt to straddle irreconcilable positions, and it involved a perpetual conflict of a
wasteful character. In all too much of his work he is engaged in
shouting down his own better judgment.

The change of front from an explicit pessimism to an apparent
optimism dates roughly from 1901 and the publication of
Anticipations. It coincides with Wells' entry into the sphere of influence of the Fabian society in political matters and of that of
William James in philosophy. James' name shows up in a list of
men recognized as great by the business State described in *When
the Sleeper Wakes*. This may suggest that Wells may have had some
doubts about his ideas at first but the reference is misleading.
Wells admired James greatly and gave Pragmatism his very
emphatically expressed approval. It is easy enough to see why,
since James' main positions are designed to plug the holes in
Huxley's Romanes lecture. Huxley's straddle involved mental
compartmentation. One part of the mind accepted the mechanistic view of the universe and one kind of truth, the other accepted
the idea of amoral order and another kind of truth to which the
first was hostile and destructive. James invented the idea of
operative truth which is supposed to cover the difficulty:

> . . . ideas (which themselves are but parts of our experience)
> become true just in so far as they help us to get into satisfactory
> relations with other parts of our experience.
>
> True ideas are those we can assimilate, validate, corroborate,
> and verify. False ideas are those we cannot.
>
> The true, to put it very briefly, is only the expedient in the way
> of our thinking, just as "the right" is only the expedient in the
> way of our behaving.

The two first of these propositions dispose of the mechanistic
view of the universe much as a lazy housemaid disposes of dust
by sweeping it under the rug. The truth about the universe which
it states neither helps us to get into satisfactory relations with

other parts of our experience nor is subject to verification. (It is possible to postulate conditions in which mind, consciousness, and experience would have no meaning, but not to verify or experience them.) The basis for pessimism therefore loses its status as truth. The last proposition deals with any realistic appreciation of human nature: it is inexpedient to consider man base, at any rate when one is trying to construct a better world, so that the idea may be dismissed as untrue.

However much these propositions may have appealed to Wells' humanitarian feelings, they grated on his æsthetic sense and his intelligence fought with them, so that it became an increasing effort to pretend that they "worked." The doubts emerge as early as 1904, in *The Food of The Gods*. This is a progressive parable about the way in which human undertakings have outgrown petty national States and their parochial administrative units. It had its genesis in a talk on Areas of Administration given at the Students' Union in the Grosvenor Road in March 1903—with Beatrice Webb in the chair. It is rounded out with a pep-talk for the new order. But, and the but is a large one, the scientists who produce the food of the Gods have no idea of what they have done. The Skinners, who put it into use in the world, are monstrous parodies of the average man, and the food produces super-rats as well as super-men and super-chickens as a result of their sloppiness and carelessness. The book is very convincing as long as it is describing how things go wrong and hardly convincing at all when it attempts to say how they will go right. What it effectively describes is the frustration and destruction of a great possibility by inferior human material. The optimism of the conclusion rests on a trick. The food of the Gods has produced a new, larger, nobler breed of human being adequate to the technological possibilities open to it, and the future rests with them. The device is transparent, and it is hard not to feel that the evasion of the real problem, of what can be done with human nature as it is, is not a conscious one. It is the first of a series of such calculated evasions. They are less apparent in the books about people than elsewhere, but they emerge from these too: *Kipps, Tono-Bungay, Ann Veronica, The History of Mr. Polly, The New Machiavelli, Marriage, The Passionate Friends,* and *The Wife of Sir Isaac Harman,* all superficially suggest that Wells is asking

the question "what shall we do with our lives" as if the answer
could be "whatever we wish." But the line of development
followed in the books shows an underlying doubt about this
answer. They show a steadily diminishing confidence in the
possibility of individual solutions. What emerges at the end of the
chain is the idea of the Mind of the Race, a group intellect which
will be freed from individual weaknesses, and which will save
humanity from its instincts. This group intellect is to be served by
semi-religious orders of devotees, the Samurai, who are to
surrender their lives to it. But at the back of this conception is an
awareness that it is not consistent with human nature that such a
surrender should in fact take place. This recognition led to Wells
writing a series of catastrophe books, stories in which he imagines
that human nature undergoes some fundamental change that
will permit the construction of a Utopian society. The ideas of
Hobbes play a large part in these fantasies. Fear, generated by a
cosmic disaster as *In the Days of the Comet*, or by atomic war in *The
World Set Free* (1914), leads men to submit to some kind of central
world government modelled on the Common Power described in
Leviathan. But the idea of a change in human nature itself is the
sine qua non of his utopias, and in the end Wells conceded that
such a change was not within the realm of possibility. His
much-parodied *Men Like Gods* is the point of concession, and it is
odd that those who have criticized the book as representing the
unpracticality and unreality of his idealism in its extreme form
have not noticed the fact. The ideal beings which inhabit its
Utopia exist in a free zone which is not within the realm of
human reality. They are special creations like the giant children
in *The Food of The Gods* and like them they are designed to evade
the truth about human nature. They live in another universe
outside the earth's spatial scheme altogether, which is part of a
very elaborate construction indeed:

> Wonder took possession of Mr. Barnstaple's mind. That dear
> world of honesty and health was beyond the utmost boundaries of
> our space, utterly inaccessible to him now for evermore; and yet,
> as he had been told, it was but one of countless universes that
> move together in time, that lie against one another, endlessly like
> the leaves of a book. And all of them are as nothing in the endless
> multitudes of systems and dimensions that surround them. "Could
> I but rotate my arm out of the limits set to it," one of the Utopians
> had said to him. "I could thrust it into a thousand universes."

This is optimism at the last ditch, an allowance of the cold comfort of an eternal moral order somewhere in a system of plural universes wholly inaccessible to human experience. And beyond that, the construction has the effect of making the book not a debate between man-as-he-might-be and man-as-he-is, but an essentially sterile clash between reality and an unattainable ideal. At best it is a cry of distress, a plea for things to be other than they are. *Men Like Gods* is in reality an altogether pessimistic book. Read in conjunction with *The Undying Fire*, which prepared the way for it, and which is a violently expressed hymn of loathing of things as they are, it leaves no doubt that in his last writings Wells was only giving a new form to beliefs which he had held all along. *The Undying Fire* is particularly moving, to those who have any sympathy with Wells at all. It shows the pendulum of his mind swinging away from its natural despairing bent over to the side of determination to construct something better out of human opportunities and back, again and again. Men are good enough to do something better than this, he says, gesticulating at the mess of the horrible world of 1919; and something better would be worth building however briefly it were to endure—and then he swings back:

> I talk . . . I talk . . . and then a desolating sense of reality blows like a destroying gust through my mind, and my little lamp of hope blows out. . . .

These words were written when he was fifty-one, and they cannot be attributed to the loss of powers which are held to account for the tone of his writing from 1942 onwards. The difference between the two phases is that in 1919 his physical buoyancy and vitality supported his will to reject what he knew in his bones. In 1919, in *The Undying Fire*, he wrote:

> I can see nothing to redeem the waste and destruction of the last four years and the still greater waste and spiritless disorder and poverty and disease ahead of us. You will tell me that the world has learnt a lesson it could learn no other way, that we shall set up a League of Nations now and put an end to war. But on what will you set up your world League of Nations? What common foundations have you made in the last four years but ruins? Is there any common idea, any common understanding yet in the minds of men?

The utterance is a despairing one. But Wells reacted to it by
setting himself the task of attempting to fabricate the necessary
common idea. *The Outline of History* was designed to provide a
universal history which would serve as the basis for a patriotism
of humanity, as national histories serve as a basis for national
patriotism. What the book states is, not that progress is inevitable, but that minkind has a common historical background, not a
racial or a regional one. It goes on to say that given the will
mankind might, by a tremendous concerted effort, establish a
world order in which all its energy could be consumed in
constructive and creative enterprises, physical, æsthetic, and
intellectual. The pendulum swung from one extreme to the other
between 1919 and 1920; with the publication of *Men Like Gods* in
1923 it had swung right back.

If I appear to be saying that Wells was inconsistent, it cannot
be helped, inconsistency is the natural consequence of an
unresolved conflict in a writer's work or thought. Wells' inconsis-
tencies could be quite dazzling at times. I remember receiving a
kind of marriage sermon from him when I was first married in
which he made a great point of monogamy and fidelity as being
an essential to true happiness. Later on I received a number of
tongue-lashings on the subject of divorce: when I told him that I
had always thought of him as a man who had saved himself
much unhappiness by divorce, he objected that this had no
bearing on the fundamental principle. Later on we had some
violent arguments on the question of pacifism. I had read a
substantial part of *The Autocracy of Mr. Parham* in the light of a
case for pacifism, and I still find it very hard not to do so. But in
1939 I was surprised to find that Wells took the line that once the
country was at war it was the citizen's job to do what he was told
to do without argument. We had many heated discussions about
this which generally became a great deal more heated whenever
I began to defend myself with the phrase "but you said, in Mr.
Parham, that . . ." "*That* has nothing to do with it, nothing at
all. . . ." During the extremely bitter internal dispute among
the Fabians in the early nineteen-hundreds Shaw attacked Wells
on these grounds, attributing his lack of intellectual discipline to
the fact that he had such tremendous facility and rapidity of
mind that he had never had really to face any practical or

intellectual difficulty, he had always been able to dodge. This
may be so. But I am inclined to trace the trouble to the central
dilemma, and to think that inconsistency and evasion became a
habit of mind because he could never bring himself to deal with
it. He comes out with it in *Boon*:

> "And that is where I want to take you up," said Wilkins. "I
> want to suggest that the mind of the race may be just a gleam of
> conscious realization that passes from darkness to darkness. . . ."
> "No," said Boon.
> "Why not?"
> "Because I will not have it so," said Boon.

Wells was Wilkins and Boon at once, and also Hallery, the
intensely serious exponent of moral values who introduces an
almost Calvinist note into the book. It was, of course, *Boon* with
its parody of Henry James, and its harsh criticism of æsthetic
values, which finally established his reputation as a Philistine.
From *Boon* onwards he made increasingly strident attacks on
literary values which are, in my view, only partially explicable
by his sense that in the state in which the world found itself
æsthetics were a luxury for which there was not enough time. It is
my view that these attacks, which went along with his reiterated
statements that his own work had no literary value, that it was
merely journalism, attached to contemporary issues; which
would become meaningless inside a couple of decades, reflected a
troubled inner sense that there was something profoundly wrong
about his own course of development. In the end I believe, on the
strength of conversations which I had with him on the particular
subject of what he meant by Dr. Moreau, and on some related
topics, that he came to feel that a realization of the truth of the
human situation, in all its ultimate hopelessness, was much more
likely to stir men to present effort to make life more tolerable
than any pretence. He felt, or so I think, that he had made a
mistake in not quashing *Boon*'s easy sentimentality. He knew in
his bones that the æsthetes were right, and that the writer's sole
duty is to state the truth which he knows. At the close of his life,
from *The Croquet Player* onwards, he was trying to recapture the
spirit in which he had written *The Island of Dr. Moreau*, and what
haunted him, and made him exceedingly unhappy, was a tragic
sense that he had returned to the real source of what could have
been his strength too late.

All this is, of course, about the inward centre of his work. Few people have brought so much buoyant vitality to the business of living, or have exercised so stimulating an effect on their friends. He spread a spirit of pleasure about him, and he made every kind of mental activity seem to be the best of sport. Although he made a number of enemies through impatience and lack of tact he made many more friends whose friendship endured through episodes which would not have been forgiven in a lesser man, and who when all was said and done rejoiced in having known him. Beyond that close circle of people who knew him there was the larger army whose hearts were warmed by the abundant spirit and courage which emanate from his writing and which make it easy to miss the intensity of his internal struggle with his demon.

Disentanglement as a Theme
in H. G. Wells's Fiction

by Robert P. Weeks

I

In H. G. Wells's earliest published piece of fiction, *The Time Machine* (1895), a scientist describes his first journey along the fourth dimension:

> I drew a breath, set my teeth, gripped the starting lever with both hands and went off with a thud. The laboratory grew faint and hazy, then fainter and ever fainter. Tomorrow night came black, then day again, night again, day again faster and faster still. An eddying murmur filled my ears and a strange numb confusedness descended on my mind . . . .
>
> Presently I noted that the sun-belt swayed up and down, from solstice to solstice, in a minute or less, and that, consequently, my pace was over a year a minute; and minute by minute the white snow flashed across the world and vanished, and was followed by the bright, brief green of spring . . . .
>
> [These sensations] . . . merged at last into a kind of hysterical exhilaration. I remarked, indeed, a clumsy swaying of the machine, for which I was unable to account. But my mind was too confused to attend to it, so with a kind of madness growing upon me, I flung myself into futurity.[1]

After the "Time Traveller," as the hero is called, explores the future and finds it dismal, he soars backward into the remote past, and never returns. The narrator concludes his story by speculating about the Time Traveller's fate: "It may be that he

"Disentanglement as a Theme in H. G. Wells's Fiction" by Robert P. Weeks. From the *Papers of the Michigan Academy of Science, Arts, and Letters*, XXXIX (1954). Reprinted by permission of the author and the Michigan Academy.

[1] Atlantic Edition (London, 1924), p. 124.

. . . fell among the blood-drinking, hairy savages of the Age of Unpolished Stone; into the abysses of the Cretaceous Sea; or among the grotesque saurians, the huge reptilian brutes of the Jurassic times." [2]

Again and again in Wells's fiction one encounters the Time Traveller. In the science fantasies he will be a "flat" character, often nameless, who is trying to break out of the physical universe; in the comedies he will bear a Dickensian label—Hoopdriver, Kipps, Polly—and be a person who is either thrust out or who stumbles out of his social universe into a higher one; in the later novels he will bear a dignified name—Remington, Trafford, Benham—and have as his mission not merely his own escape from a limiting environment but the liberation of his society or of the entire planet.

It is my purpose to direct attention to the special world created in Wells's fiction and peopled by these figures. It is a world enclosed by a network of limitations and dominated by the image of a man driven by a profound and, at times, an irrational desire to escape. Although the network appears at first to be impenetrable, the hero finally succeeds in disentangling himself. This action invariably creates in him "a kind of hysterical exhilaration." But ultimately he experiences defeat in the form either of disillusionment or of death.

Wells's novels are today commonly regarded as the disorderly transcript of an opportunistic mind constantly grubbing for "topics." I believe it can be demonstrated, however, that his work has a meaningful coherence and unity. But one of the chief difficulties of such an enterprise is the size of Wells's output—he wrote nearly fifty novels. To minimize this difficulty, I shall limit myself in this paper to his science fantasies—both because they are a manageable segment of his work and because they have considerable "solidity of specification," a particularly desirable quality when one is looking for landmarks in a writer's special world. I have tried to point out, so far as space will permit, resemblances between the fantasies and Wells's other fiction.[3]

---

[2] *Ibid.,* p. 205.

[3] I have attempted the same sort of analysis of all of his fiction elsewhere—see "H. G. Wells as a Sociological Novelist" (unpublished doctoral dissertation, University of Michigan, 1952).

The first counterpart of the Time Traveller appears in *The Island of Doctor Moreau* (1896), Wells's second published work. This is the story of a grisly, unfeeling surgeon, Moreau, who attempts by means of plastic and neurosurgery to give his bears, dogs, and gorillas the bodies and minds of men. When they begin to walk and talk like men he exults in his godlike power to direct and accelerate the process of evolution. As the creator of these "beast people" he even hands down to them a moral code that has such commandments as: "Not to go on all-fours; that is the law. Are we not men? Not to suck up drink; that is the law. Are we not men?" But Dr. Moreau's experiment is cut short when one of his protégés brutally murders him. Without their "god" to drive them, the beast people fall back on all fours and regress to their appropriate moment in biological time.

Like Dr. Moreau, the albino, Griffin, in *The Invisible Man* (1897), becomes a monomaniac in his struggle to overcome the laws of optics. He throws over his teaching career and kills his father for money because of his insane obsession with "the magnificent vision of all that invisibility might mean to a man—the mystery, the power, the freedom." But, for all his inhumanity, Griffin momentarily becomes human when he experiences the exultation of his triumph over physical law. He destroys his laboratory, tears off his clothing, and strides out into the traffic of Oxford Street completely invisible and full of "a feeling of extraordinary elation." In those few moments Griffin enjoys that perfect euphoria that Wells's characters always experience when they have crashed through some barrier that has restrained them. Mr. Polly had the same feeling of blissful release when he walked away from his nagging wife; Uncle Teddy Ponderevo felt it when he escaped from his bankrupt, small-town pharmacy to London, where he made Tono-Bungay "zoom"; and Ann Veronica felt it when she defied conventional morality by running off with her married zoology instructor.

Disentanglement takes the form of space travel in *The War of the Worlds* (1898) and *The First Men in the Moon* (1901). Escaping into space carried with it the same deadly penalty as breaking out of the time continuum or violating the laws of evolution or optics. For example, the Martians, who through the exercise of extreme ingenuity and courage were able to traverse interplanetary space, are ironically destroyed in *The War of the Worlds* by the action of earthly bacteria that are harmless to men. Wells returned to biology in the last of his early science fantasies, *The Food of the Gods* (1904). In this story an organic chemist finds that plants and animals do not grow steadily, but in spurts. He discovers the hormone-like substance responsible for these spurts and feeds it first to animals and then to some children, who grow into forty-foot giants. Their size enables them to escape the petty entanglements of "the little people," but they enjoy their liberation only briefly. The little people, who fear and hate them, ultimately destroy them.

After he abandoned the science-fantasy form in 1904, to direct most of his attention to other forms of the novel, Wells did not drop the theme of disentanglement. The image of the Time Traveller throwing himself with hysterical exhilaration against the barriers of his environment appears again and again in the later novels, just as it did in the fantasies. The Wellsian man is endowed with a free will and an instinctive craving for freedom whether he is a scientist bound for the moon or a bankrupt shopkeeper deserting his nagging wife. None of Wells's novels is built around a character like Arnold Bennett's Constance Baines, who moves smoothly and unobtrusively through life. Wells's characters do not passively submit to time, nor do they, like the characters in naturalistic novels, automatically respond to their milieus. Least of all are they Mrs. Dalloways, floating in currents of memory and momentary sensory perceptions that they allow to flow through and around them. Wells's protagonists, in both his fantasies and his other novels, look on their environment as a series of barriers that somehow must be broken through.

II

Whenever a writer creates a special world in his fiction there is always the possibility that he is imitating other writers and adopting their conventions. But the world of Wells's fantasies was not a convention of the nineteenth-century science fantasy. Jules Verne's fiction, for example, does not display any consistent tendency to depict characters being ecstatically catapulted over earthly barriers. Instead of being energized in this way, Verne's characters—like Captain Nemo, the submariner in *Twenty Thousand Leagues under the Sea* (1870)—are inclined to accept all the restrictions of their environment and to work *within* them.

If it cannot be explained as imitation of other writers, Wells's concern with disentanglement can be explained, in part, as a reaction to science. Wells's exposure to science was probably as thorough as that of any English novelist. He studied biology under Huxley, took first-class honors in zoology, taught college courses in biology, and wrote science textbooks. But his interest in science was more than academic. He was keenly aware of its social and philosophical implications and possibilities. From his earliest published essay, in 1891, until his death in 1946, Wells was deeply concerned with the promise of science to help man understand and improve his environment. In his first essay, "The Rediscovery of the Unique" (1891), he compares science to a match. Man has struck it with the hope and expectation that it will light up the dark room in which he stands, but he finds that it throws only a flickering and momentary glow on his hands and face, leaving the rest of the room in almost complete blackness. In more florid pieces, like *A Modern Utopia* (1905) and *The Shape of Things to Come* (1933), science is not so much a flickering match as a beacon. However, the attitude toward science that appears in Wells's pronouncements on it, taken in bulk, is faith in it as a good tool, but faith moderated by skepticism about man's ability to obtain a knowledge of final reality with this tool or any other now available to him.

In his fiction, Wells's characters display great confidence in the power of science to achieve their particular utopias, but this confidence is invariably shown to be excessive, or at least premature. It is characteristic of the Wells novel that during the first three quarters of the story the characters act as if the match will light up the universe, whereas in the last pages it merely burns their hands. Yet this is never interpreted as an argument against matches. After all, Wells would ask, what else is there?

One of the dangers in trying to reach any general conclusions about Wells's fiction by an examination of his science fantasies is that too much importance will be assigned to the role of science. In the special world created by Wells, I have tried to show that the central image is of man trapped by his environment. In the fantasies man breaks free through the fantastic use of science, but in the other novels various devices are used, although science is usually preferred.

What is more fundamental to Wells's work than a concern with science is his invariable habit of depicting human life as an unsuccessful struggle to escape. His interest in science explains his choice of it as the favorite instrument for escape, but this interest does not adequately explain why his characters exist in that kind of a world in the first place. Perhaps the most likely reason for Wells's having created the special world he did is the rigidly stratified Victorian society into which he was born—the son of an estate gardener and a lady's maid—and to whose upper levels he beat his way, becoming one of the most widely read publicists and novelists of our time.

But although it is certainly worth while to try to establish the inner reason for a writer's choice of characters and situations, a more ˗fundamental, and necessarily antecedent, activity is the discovery of the sort of world he has created in his fiction. My purpose has been to point out that Wells's fiction—of which the science fantasies are representative—presents us with a unified world that limits its inhabitants, provokes their rebellion, and then frustrates their flight, in spite of the energy, ingenuity, and daring with which it is undertaken. The recurrence of this world is the answer to those who accuse Wells of presenting in each successive novel a message that canceled his previous message.[4] Its existence is useful also in countering the charge that Wells preached that man was "progressing through science to Utopia,"[5] or that he used science in his fiction as a magic staircase offering a way out of difficult social problems.[6] It is true that Wells's fiction appears to be charged with optimism. V. S. Pritchett has remarked that when he begins a novel by Wells he experiences "an exhilarating sense of personal freedom." Many critics have testified to this power. But when the time machines crash, the invisible men are tracked down, and the beast people fall back on all fours, this sense of freedom is shown to have been

[4] See Stuart Pratt Sherman, "The Utopian Naturalism of H. G. Wells," in Sherman, *On Contemporary Literature* (New York, 1917), p. 81.

[5] "Journalism and Joachim's Children," *Time*, 61 (March 9, 1953): 59.

[6] V. S. Pritchett, *The Living Novel* (London, 1946), p. 119. ["The Scientific Romances" from this book is the next chapter in this volume.—Ed.]

somewhat illusory, because the optimism was excessive. Yet this optimism is not of a wholly unstable kind that collapses at the end of the narrative into bleak despair. It becomes transformed, true enough, but into the sort of tough hopefulness with which the narrator responds to the Time Traveller's dismal picture of the future: "If that is so, it remains for us to live as though it were not so."

The tension in Wells's fiction between excessive optimism and chastened optimism, between promise and threat, and between fulfillment and defeat is accurately reflected in what are probably the most widely quoted words he ever wrote: "Human history becomes more and more a race between education and catastrophe." Wells's greatness as a social and political thinker resulted primarily from the manner in which the world he constructed in his novels has clarified and ordered and stimulated our thinking about the changing, complicated world of the twentieth century. And his decline as a novelist resulted from his unfortunate tendency more and more to argue about the world in which he lived rather than to render it. But at any rate an awareness of the nature of the special world he created is indispensable to an understanding of his fiction.

The Scientific Romances

by V. S. Pritchett

A cloud of dust travels down the flinty road and chokes the
glossy Kentish greenery. From the middle of the moving cloud
come the ejaculations of an unhandy driver; the clopper of
horses' hooves, the rumble of a wagonette or trap. One catches
the flash of a top-hat or a boater. One smells horse manure and
beer. And one hears that peculiar English spoken by the lower
middle class, a language in which the syllable "-ing" either
becomes "-ink" or loses its final "g," and which is enlivened by
cries of "Crikey" and "Golly." The accent is despairing,
narrow-vowelled yet truculent, with something of the cheap-jack
and Sunday League in it, and it is broken by a voice, not quite so
common which says things like, "We're not the finished thing.
We're jest one of Nature's experiments, see. We're jest the
beginning." And then—I don't quite know why—there is a
crash. Over goes the wagonette, the party inside hit out with
their fists, noses bleed, eyes are blackened. Most surprising, a
nearby house catches fire. Do not be alarmed. The time is the
late 'nineties and you have simply been watching the outing of a
group of early H. G. Wells characters who have become suddenly
aware that science is radically changing the human environment. No Frenchified or Russianised fiction this, but plain,
cheerful, vulgar, stoic, stupid and hopelessly romantic English. It
is as English as the hoardings.

There are always fist-fights and fires in the early Wells. Above
all, there are fires. They occur, as far as I remember, in all the
scientific romances except *The Island of Dr. Moreau*—a very

pessimistic book—and are an ingredient of the Wellsian optimism, an optimism whose other name, I fear, is ruthlessness. I
have lately read all those scientific books from *The Time Machine*
to *The War in the Air* and it has been a refreshing experience.
There was a time, one realises, when science was fun. For the
food of the gods is more entertaining than the prosaic efficacity of
vitamins; the tripods of the Martians are more engaging than
tanks. And then, here you have Wells at his best, eagerly
displaying the inventive imagination, first with the news and at
play, with an artist's innocence. Here you see his intoxicated
response—a response that was lacking in his contemporaries—to
the front-page situation of his time, and here you meet his
mastery of the art of story-telling, the bounce and resource of it.
Above all, in these early books, you catch Wells in the act, his
very characteristic act, of breaking down mean barriers and
setting you free. He has burst out himself and he wants everyone
else to do the same. "Why," cries the engineer in *The Food of the
Gods*—the poorest of these books—"Why don't we do what we
want to do?"

For that matter, I have never read any book by H. G. Wells,
early or late, which did not start off by giving me an exhilarating
sense of personal freedom. Every inhibition I ever had faded from
me as I read. Of course, after such a high, hard bounce one
comes down again. The answer to the engineer's question is that
we do not do what we want to do because we want to do opposite
things at the same time. Yet that infectious Wellsian sense of
freedom was not all anarchy, romantic ebullience or Utopian
uplift. That freedom was a new fact in our environment; one
pays for everything—that is all. I do not know what date is given
to the second scientific revolution, but one has to go back to the
great centuries of geographical discovery for a comparable
enlargement of our world; and it is a suggestive fact that we have
to go back to Swift, the Swift of Lilliput and Laputa, before
we find another English novelist going to science for his data
and material as Wells has done. (The influence of science, in the
150 years that lie between those two writers, is philosophical, not
factual.) Wells's eager recognition of the new environment is one
of the sources of the sense of freedom we get from him. I make no
comparison of the merits of Wells and Swift—though the
Beast-Men of *The Island of Dr. Moreau* are derivatives of the

Yahoos and are observed with Swift's care for biological detail—
but in his best narratives Wells does go back to the literary
traditions of the early eighteenth century, the highest traditions
of our narrative literature. The ascendancy of Swift is a question
of imaginative range and style; above all it is due to a humanity
which is denied to Wells because he arrived at the beginning, the
crude beginning, of a new enlargement, whereas Swift arrived
towards the end of one. None of Wells's narrators, whether they
are South Kensington scientists or people, like the awful Bert,
who appear to be suffering from an emotional and linguistic
toothache, is capable of the philosophical simplicity and sanity of
Gulliver; for Wells has only just spotted this new world of
agitating chemicals, peculiar glands, and obliterating machines.
The sense of wonder has not grown far beyond a sense of copy.
He is topical and unstable, swept by eagerness yet visited by
nauseas sudden and horrifying. Suppose we evolve into futility or
revert to the beast from which we have arisen? Such speculations
are alien to the orthodox eyes which were set in Swift's mad
head; he had no eye to the future; the eighteenth century
believed in a static world. The things Swift sees *have happened*. To
Wells—and how typical of an expanding age—the things he sees
have *not* happened. They are possibilities. In these scientific
romances one catches occasionally the humane and settled note:
in *The Time Machine*, in *The Island of Dr. Moreau* and in *The War of
the Worlds*, which are the most imaginative stories of the group
and are free of the comic Edwardian horseplay. The practical
experiment has been detached from the practical joke; the idea is
untainted by the wheeze. The opening sentence of *The War of the
Worlds* suggests a settled view of humanity, besides being an
excellent example of Wells's mastery of the art of bouncing us
into belief in anything he likes to tell us:

> No one would have believed in the last years of the nineteenth
> century that human affairs were being watched keenly and closely
> by intelligences greater than man's and yet as mortal as his own.

It is not surprising that the passages of low comedy, which
elsewhere are Wells's excellence, should be a failure in the
scientific romances. Naturally they break the spell of the illusion
with their clumsy realism. And if love is born, Wells is Walt
Disney at his worst. The love scenes between the giants in *The*

Food of the Gods are the most embarrassing in English fiction, and one wonders that the picture of the awful Princess, goggling in enormous close-up and fanning herself with half a chestnut tree, did not destroy the feminist movement. But except for faint squirms of idyllic petting in *The Time Machine*, none of these aberrations misdirects the narratives of the three books I have mentioned. I cannot include *The War in the Air* among the best; it *is* an astonishing piece of short-term prophecy and judgment. One remembers the bombing of battleships and the note on the untroubled minds of those who bomb one another's cities; but the book is below Wells's highest level. So, too, is *The Invisible Man*, which is a good thriller, but it develops jerkily and is held up by horseplay and low comedy. Without question *The Time Machine* is the best piece of writing. It will take its place among the great stories of our language. Like all excellent works it has meanings within its meaning and no one who has read the story will forget the dramatic effect of the change of scene in the middle of the book, when the story alters its key, and the Time Traveller reveals the foundation of slime and horror on which the pretty life of his Arcadians is precariously and fearfully resting. I think it is fair to accuse the later Wells of escaping into a dream world of plans, of using science as a magic staircase out of essential social problems. I think the best Wells is the destructive, ruthless, black-eye-dealing and house-burning Wells who foresaw the violence and not the order of our time. However this may be, the early Wells of *The Time Machine* did not escape. The Arcadians had become as pretty as flowers in their pursuit of personal happiness. They had dwindled and would be devoured because of that. Their happiness itself was haunted. Here Wells's images of horror are curious. The slimy, the viscous, the foetal reappear; one sees the sticky, shapeless messes of pond life, preposterous in instinct and frighteningly without mind. One would like to hear a psychologist on these shapes which recall certain surrealist paintings; but perhaps the biologist fishing among the algæ, and not the unconscious, is responsible for them. In *The Time Machine*—and also in the other two books—Wells is aware of pain. None of his investigators returns without wounds and bruises to the mind as well as the body, and Dr. Moreau is, of course, a sadist. *The Island* is hard on the nerves and displays a horror more definite and calculated than anything in Wells's other books. Where *The Time Machine* relieves us by its poetic social allegory, *The Island of Dr. Moreau* takes us into an abyss of human nature. We are left naked at the end of the shocking report, looking with apprehension at the bodies of our friends, imagining the tell-tale short legs, the eyes that shine green in the dark, the reversion to the wolf, the hyena, the monkey and the dog. This book is a superb piece of story-telling from our first sight of the unpleasant ship and its stinking, mangy menagerie, to the last malign episode where the narrator is left alone on the island with the Beast-Men. Neither Dr. Moreau nor his drunken assistant is a lay figure and, in that last episode, the Beast-Men become creatures of Swiftian malignance:

> The Monkey Man bored me, however. He assumed, on the strength of his five digits, that he was my equal, and was forever jabbering at me, jabbering the most arrant nonsense. One thing about him entertained me a little: he had a fantastic trick of coining new words. He had an idea, I believe, that to gabble about names that meant nothing was the proper use of speech. He called it "big thinks," to distinguish it from "little thinks"—the sane everyday interests of life. If ever I made a remark he did not understand, he would praise it very much, ask me to say it again, learn it by heart, and go off repeating it, with a word wrong here and there, to all the wilder of the Beast People. He thought nothing of what was plain and comprehensible. I invented some very curious "big thinks" for his especial use.

The description of the gradual break in the morale of the Beast-Men is a wonderful piece of documented guesswork. It is easy enough to be sensational. It is quite another matter to domesticate the sensational. One notices, too, how Wells's idea comes full circle in his best thrillers. There is the optimistic outward journey, there is the chastened return.

It would be interesting to know more about the origins of *The Island of Dr. Moreau*, for they must instruct us on the pessimism and the anarchy which lie at the heart of Wells's ebullient nature. This is the book of a wounded man who has had a sight of sadism and death. The novelist who believed in the cheerful necessity of evolution is halted by the thought of its disasters and losses. Perhaps man is unteachable. It is exciting and emancipating to believe we are one of nature's latest experiments, but what if the experiment is unsuccessful? What if it is unsurmountably unpleasant? Suppose the monkey drives the machine, the gullible, mischievous, riotous and irresponsible monkey? It is an interesting fact that none of Wells's optimistic contemporaries considered such a possibility. Shaw certainly did not. Evil, in Shaw, is curable. He believes in the Protestant effort. He believes that men *argue* their way along the path of evolution, and that the life force is always on the side of the cleverest mind and the liveliest conscience. When he reflects on the original monkey, Shaw cannot resist the thought that the monkey was a shrewd animal going up in the world, and Shaw feels a patronising pride in him which the self-made man may feel about the humble ancestor who gave him his start in life. There is certainly no suggestion that he will ever lose his capital, which is civilisation, and revert. There is no thought, in this quintessential Irish Protestant, that the original monkey may be original sin. Nor could there be: the doctrine of original sin is a device of the emotions, and about our emotions Shaw knows absolutely nothing at all. But to the emotional Wells, the possibility of original sin in the form of the original monkey is always present. The price of progress may be perversion and horror, and Wells is honest enough to accept that. Shaw appears to think we can evade all painful issues by a joke, just as Chesterton, the Catholic optimist of his generation, resolved serious questions by a series of puns.

Wells can be wounded. It is one of his virtues. One is reminded of Kipling, another wounded writer—was Wells satirising Kipling in that chapter of *The Island of Dr. Moreau* where the Beast-Men are seen mumbling their pathetic Law?—and Kipling and Wells are obviously divergent branches of the same tree. Wells the Utopian, Kipling the patriot—they represent the day-dreams of the lower middle class which will either turn to socialism or fascism. Opposed in tendency, Wells and Kipling both have the vision of artists; they foresee the conditions of our time. They both foretell the violence with a certain appetite. Crudity appeals to them. They are indifferent or bad-hearted, in human relations. They understand only personal independence which, from time to time, in their work is swallowed up in mass relationships. In the final count, Kipling—like Wells's man in the sewer in *The War of the Worlds*—falls back on animal cunning. It is the knowing, tricky, crafty animal that survives by lying low and saying nothing. Kipling, for all his admiration of power, believes in the neurotic, the morbid and defeated mind. This strain is in Wells also, but he has more private stoicism than Kipling has, a stoicism which blossoms from time to time into a belief in miracles and huge strokes of luck. Impatient of detail, mysteriously reticent about the immediate practical steps we must take to ensure any of his policies, Wells believes—like Kipling —in magic: a magic induced by impudence or rebellion. Wells and Kipling—these two are light and shadow to each other.

Wells's achievement was that he installed the paraphernalia of our new environment in our imagination; and life does not become visible or tolerable to us until artists have assimilated it. We do not need to read beyond these early scientific works of his to realise what he left out. The recent war, whose conditions he so spryly foresaw, has made that deficiency clear. When we read those prophetic accounts of mechanised warfare and especially of air bombardment, we must be struck by one stupendous misreading of the future. It occurs where we should expect it to occur: in the field of *morale*. Wells imagined cities destroyed and the inhabitants flying in terror. He imagined the soldiers called out to keep order and the conditions of martial law and total anarchy. He imagined mass terror and riot. He did not reckon with the nature, the moral resources, the habits of civilised man. Irresponsible himself, he did not attribute anything but an obstructive value to human responsibility. That is a serious deficiency, for it indicates an ignorance of the rooted, inner life of men and women, a jejune belief that we live by events and programmes; but how, in the heyday of a great enlargement of the human environment, could he believe otherwise? We turn back to our Swift and there we see a mad world also; but it is a mad world dominated by the sober figure of the great Gulliver, that plain, humane figure. Not a man of exquisite nor adventurous spirituality; not a great soul; not a man straining all his higher faculties to produce some new mutation; not a man trying to blow himself out like the frog of the fable to the importunate dimensions of his programme; but, quite simply, a man. Endowed with curiosity, indeed, but empowered by reserve. Anarchists like Wells, Kipling, Shaw and the pseudo-orthodox Chesterton, had no conception of such a creature. They were too fascinated by their own bombs.

The Time Machine:
An Ironic Myth

by Bernard Bergonzi

H. G. Wells seems so essentially a writer of the first half of
the twentieth century that we tend to forget that if he had died in
1900 at the age of thirty-four he would already have had a dozen
books to his credit. He first established his reputation by the
scientific romances written during these early years of his literary
career, and they have remained popular. Historically considered,
they are of interest as the forerunners of much latter-day science
fiction. Yet, in my opinion, more substantial claims can be made
for them. They are often compared with the work of Jules Verne,
but this is a misleading comparison even if a plausible one. Wells
himself wrote in 1933, "there is no resemblance whatever
between the anticipatory inventions of the great Frenchman and
these fantasies." His early romances, in fact, despite their air of
scientific plausibility, are much more works of pure imagination.
They are, in short, *fantasies,* and the emphasis should be on
"romance" rather than "scientific." And like other kinds of
literary romance they are distinguished by a quality which may
reasonably be called symbolic, even if not specifically allegorical.
Indeed, I would claim that Wells's early fiction is closer to the
symbolic romances of Hawthorne or Melville, or to a complex
fantasy like *Dr. Jekyll and Mr. Hyde,* or even to the fables of Kafka,
than it is to the more strictly scientific speculations of Verne.
This at least, is the assumption on which I base the following

"*The Time Machine:* An Ironic Myth" by Bernard Bergonzi. From *Critical
Quarterly*, II (Winter 1960). Included in revised form in Bernard Bergonzi, *The
Early H. G. Wells* (Manchester: Manchester University Press and Toronto:
Toronto University Press, 1961). Copyright © 1960, 1961 by Bernard Bergonzi.
Reprinted by permission of the author.

examination of *The Time Machine*, Wells's first novel, which appeared in 1895. This approach has already been hinted at by one of the best of Wells's modern critics, V. S. Pritchett, who has written:

> Without question *The Time Machine* is the best piece of writing. It will take its place among the great stories of our language. Like all excellent works it has meanings within its meaning . . .[1]

An earlier writer on Wells, Edward Shanks, remarked:

> If I were to say that many of Mr. Wells's early books have a poetic quality I should run the risk of conveying a false impression. Luckily they have a peculiar quality which enables them to bear a special description. They are, in their degree, myths; and Mr. Wells is a mythmaker.[2]

Shanks expanded his remarks with particular reference to *The Island of Dr. Moreau*, though they apply equally to *The Time Machine*:

> These passages suggest one interpretation of the book. But it is a myth, not an allegory; and whereas an allegory bears a single and definite interpretation, a myth does not, but can be interpreted in many ways, none of them quite consistent, all of them more alive and fruitful than the rigid allegorical correspondence.

Pritchett has referred to *The Time Machine* as a "poetic social allegory." But this narrows the effective range of the work too much; though on one level the "allegory," or in Shanks's more appropriate term, the "myth," does operate in social terms, its further significance is biological and even cosmological. Structurally, *The Time Machine* belongs to the class of story which includes James's *Turn of the Screw*, and which Northrop Frye has called "the tale told in quotation marks, where we have an opening setting with a small group of congenial people, and then the real story told by one of the members." As Frye observes:

> The effect of such devices is to present the story through a relaxed and contemplative haze as something that entertains us without, so to speak, confronting us, as direct tragedy confronts us.[3]

[1] *The Living Novel* (London, 1946), pp. 119–20.
[2] *First Essays on Literature* (London, 1923), p. 158.
[3] *Anatomy of Criticism* (Princeton, 1957), p. 202.

The aesthetic distancing of the central narrative of *The Time Machine*, "the time traveller's story," is carefully carried out. At the end of the book, the traveller says:

> "No, I cannot expect you to believe it. Take it as a lie—or a prophecy. Say I dreamed it in the workshop. Consider I have been speculating upon the destinies of our race, until I have hatched this fiction. Treat my assertion of its truth as a mere stroke of art to enhance its interest. And taking it as a story, what do you think of it?"

The manifest disbelief of all his friends other than the story-teller—one of them "thought the tale a 'gaudy lie' "—is balanced by the apparent evidence of his sojourn in the future, the "two strange white flowers" of an unknown species. In fact, Wells demands assent by apparently discouraging it.

The opening chapters of the novel show us the inventor entertaining his friends, a group of professional men, in the solid comfort of his home at Richmond. They recall the "club-man" atmosphere with which several of Kipling's short stories open, and their function in the narrative is to give it a basis in contemporary life at its most ordinary and pedestrian: this atmosphere makes the completest possible contrast with what is to come: an account of a wholly imaginative world of dominantly paradisal and demonic imagery, lying far outside the possible experience of the late Victorian bourgeoisie. These chapters are essential to Wells's purpose, since they prevent the central narrative from seeming a piece of pure fantasy, or a fairy story, and no more. The character of the time traveller himself—cheerful, erratic, and somewhat absurd, faintly suggestive of a hero of Jerome K. Jerome's—has a similar function. In the work of other popular writers of fantastic romance in the nineties, such as Arthur Machen and M. P. Shiel (both clearly deriving from Stevenson), a "weird" atmosphere is striven after from the very beginning and the dramatic power is correspondingly less.

Once the reader has been initiated into the group of friends, he is prepared for whatever is to come next. First the model time machine is produced—"a glittering metallic framework, scarcely larger than a small clock, and very delicately made. . . . There was ivory in it, and some crystalline substance"—and sent off into time, never to be seen again. Then we are shown the full scale machine, and the account of it is a brilliant example of Wells's impressionistic method:

> "I remember vividly the flickering light, his queer, broad head in silhouette, the dance of the shadows, how we all followed him, puzzled but incredulous, and how there in the laboratory we beheld a larger edition of the little mechanism which we had seen vanish from before our eyes. Parts were of nickel, parts of ivory, parts had certainly been filed or sawn out of rock crystal. The thing was generally complete, but the twisted crystalline bars lay unfinished upon the bench besides some sheets of drawings, and I took one up for a better look at it. Quartz it seemed to be."

The assemblage of details is strictly speaking meaningless but nevertheless conveys very effectively a sense of the machine without putting the author to the taxing necessity of giving a direct description.

The central narrative of *The Time Machine* is of a kind common to several of Wells's early romances: a central character is transferred to or marooned in a wholly alien environment, and the story arises from his efforts to deal with the situation. This is the case with the time traveller, with the angel in *The Wonderful Visit* and with Prendick in *The Island of Dr. Moreau*, while Griffin in *The Invisible Man* becomes the victim of his environment in attempting to control it. Though Wells is a writer of symbolic fiction—or a myth-maker—the symbolism is not of the specifically heraldic kind that we associate, for instance, with Hawthorne's scarlet letter, Melville's white whale, or James's golden bowl. In Wells the symbolic element is inherent in the total fictional situation, rather more in the manner of Kafka. When, for instance, we are shown in *The Time Machine* a paradisal world on the surface of the earth inhabited by beautiful carefree beings leading a wholly aesthetic existence, and a diabolic or demonic world beneath the surface inhabited by brutish creatures who spend most of their time in darkness in underground machine shops, and only appear on the surface at night, and when we are told that these two races are the descendents respectively of the present-day bourgeoisie and proletariat, and that the latter live by cannibalistically preying on the former—then clearly we are faced with a symbolic situation of considerable complexity, where several different "mythical" interpretations are possible.

The time traveller—unlike his predecessor, Nebogipfel (hero of *The Chronic Argonauts*, Wells's first version of *The Time Machine*, published in a student magazine in 1888), and his successors, Moreau and Griffin—is not a solitary eccentric on the Franken-stein model, but an amiable and gregarious bourgeois. Like Wells himself, he appears to be informed and interested in the dominant intellectual movements of his age, Marxism and Darwinism. Wells had come across Marx at South Kensington, and though in later years he was to become extremely anti-Marxist, in his immediate post-student days he was prepared to uphold Marxian socialism as "a new thing based on Darwinism." However doubtfully historical this may be, the juxtaposition of the two names is very important for Wells's early imaginative and speculative writing. The time traveller, immediately after he has arrived in the world of 802701, is full of forebodings about the kind of humanity he may discover:

> What might not have happened to men? What if cruelty had grown into a common passion? What if in this interval the race had lost its manliness, and had developed into something inhuman, unsympathetic, and overwhelmingly powerful? I might seem some old-world savage animal, only the more dreadful and disgusting for our common likeness—a foul creature to be incontinently slain.

At first, however, his more fearful speculations are not fulfilled. Instead of what he had feared, he discovers the Eloi, who are small, frail and beautiful. He is rather shocked and then amused by their child-like ways and manifest lack of intellectual powers—"the memory of my confident anticipations of a pro-foundly grave and intellectual posterity came, with irresistible merriment, to my mind." Such a "grave and intellectual posterity" had in fact been postulated by Bulwer Lytton in *The Coming Race*, 1871, a work, which it has been suggested had some influence on *The Time Machine*, though the resemblances are very slight. But it is quite possible that Wells was here alluding to Bulwer Lytton's romance, as well as to the wider implications of optimistic evolutionary theory.

Subsequently the traveller becomes charmed with the Eloi and the relaxed communism of their way of life. They live, not in

separate houses, but in large semi-ruinous buildings of considerable architectural splendour, sleeping and eating there commu-
nally. Their only food is fruit, which abounds in great richness
and variety, and they are described in a way which suggests the
figures of traditional pastoral poetry: "They spent all their time
in playing gently, in bathing in the river, in making love in a
half-playful fashion, in eating fruit and sleeping." Later the
traveller takes stock of their world:

> I have already spoken of the great palaces dotted about among
> the variegated greenery, some in ruins and some still occupied.
> Here and there rose a white silvery figure in the waste garden of
> the earth, here and there came the sharp vertical line of some
> cupola or obelisk. There were no hedges, no signs of proprietary
> rights, no evidences of agriculture; the whole earth had become a
> garden.

There appear to be no animals, wild or domestic, left in the
world, and such forms of life as remain have clearly been subject
to a radical process of selection:

> The air was free from gnats, the earth from weeds or fungi;
> everywhere were fruits and sweet and delightful flowers; brilliant
> butterflies flew hither and thither. The ideal of preventive
> medicine was attained. Disease had been stamped out. I saw no
> evidence of any contagious diseases during all my stay. And I
> shall have to tell you later that even the processes of putrefaction
> and decay had been profoundly affected by these changes.

Man has, in short, at some period long past obtained complete
control of his environment, and has been able to manipulate the
conditions of life to his absolute satisfaction. The "struggle for
existence" has been eliminated, and as a result of this manipula-
tion the nature of the species has undergone profound modification. Not only have the apparent physical differences between
male and female disappeared, but their mental powers have
declined as well as their physical. The human race, as it presents
itself to the traveller, is plainly in its final decadence. The Eloi,
with their childlike and sexually ambiguous appearance, and
their consumptive type of beauty, are clearly reflections of *fin de
siècle* visual taste. *The Time Machine* is in several respects a book of
its time, for speculations about decadence and degeneration were

much in the air in the eighties and early nineties, reaching their peak in Max Nordau's massive work of destructive criticism, *Degeneration*. Wells certainly knew the English edition of this book, which appeared in March 1895, when *The Time Machine* was already completed, for he makes a satirical reference to it in his second novel, *The Wonderful Visit*, published the following October.

In the world that the traveller surveys, aesthetic motives have evidently long been dominant as humanity has settled down to its decline. "This has ever been the fate of energy in security; it takes to art and to eroticism, and then comes languour and decay." But in the age of the Eloi even artistic motives seem almost extinct. "To adorn themselves with flowers, to dance, to sing in the sunlight; so much was left to the artistic spirit, and no more." The implied comment on *fin de siècle* aestheticism is, again, unmistakable. The first chapter of the time traveller's narrative is called "In the Golden Age," and the following chapter, "The Sunset of Mankind": there is an ironic effect, not only in the juxtaposition, but in the very reference to a "golden age." Such an age, the *Saturnia regna*, when men were imagined as living a simple, uncomplicated and happy existence, before in some way falling from grace, was always an object of literary nostalgia, and traditionally thought of as being at the very beginning of man's history. Wells, however, places it in the remotest future, and associates it not with dawn but with sunset. The time traveller sees the Eloi as leading a paradisal existence, and his sense of this is imparted to the reader by the imagery of the first part of his narrative. They are thoroughly assimilated to their environment, where "the whole earth had become a garden," and "everywhere were fruits and sweet and delicious flowers; brilliant butterflies flew hither and thither." Their appearance and mode of life makes a pointed contrast to the drab and earnest figure of the traveller:

> Several more brightly-clad people met me in the doorway, and so we entered, I, dressed in dingy nineteenth-century garments, looking grotesque enough, garlanded with flowers, and surrounded by an eddying mass of bright, soft-coloured robes and shining white limbs, in a melodious whirl of laughter and laughing speech.

The writing here suggests that Wells was getting a little out of his depth, but the intention is clearly to present the Eloi as in some sense heirs to Pre-Raphaelite convention. This implicit contrast between the aesthetic and the utilitarian, the beautiful and idle set against the ugly and active, shows how *The Time Machine* embodies another profound late-Victorian preoccupation, re-calling, for instance, the aesthetic anti-industrialism of Ruskin and Morris. The world of the Eloi is presented as not only a golden age, but as something of a lotos land, and it begins to exercise its spell on the traveller. After his immediate panic on discovering the loss of his machine, he settles down to a philosophic resignation:

> Suppose the worst? I said. Suppose the machine altogether lost—perhaps destroyed? It behoves me to be calm and patient, to learn the way of the people, to get a clear idea of the method of my loss, and the means of getting materials and tools; so that in the end, perhaps, I may make another. That would be my only hope, a poor hope, perhaps, but better than despair. And, after all, it was a beautiful and curious world.

The traveller's potential attachment to the Eloi and their world is strengthened when he rescues the little female, Weena, from drowning, and begins a prolonged flirtation with her. This relationship is the biggest flaw in the narrative, for it is totally unconvincing, and tends to embarrass the reader (Pritchett has referred to the "faint squirms of idyllic petting.") But though the traveller feels the attraction of the kind of life she represents, he is still too much a man of his own age, resourceful, curious and active, to succumb to it. As he says of himself, "I am too Occidental for a long vigil. I could work at a problem for years, but to wait inactive for twenty-four hours—that is another matter."

But it is not long before he becomes aware that the Eloi are not the only forms of animal life left in the world, and his curiosity is once more aroused. He realises that Weena and the Eloi generally have a great fear of darkness: "But she dreaded the dark, dreaded shadows, dreaded black things." Here we have the first hint of the dominant imagery of the second half of the narrative, the darkness characteristic of the Morlocks, and the ugly, shapeless forms associated with it, contrasting with the light and the brilliant colours of the Eloi and their world. Looking into the darkness one night just before dawn the traveller imagines that he can see vague figures running across the landscape, but cannot be certain whether or not his eyes have deceived him. And a little later, when he is exploring one of the ruined palaces, he comes across a strange creature—"a queer little ape-like figure" that runs away from him and disappears down one of the well-like shafts that are scattered across the country, and whose purpose and nature had puzzled the traveller on his arrival: "My impression of it is, of course, imperfect; but I know it was a dull white, and had strange large greyish-red eyes; also that there was flaxen hair on its head and down its back." The traveller now has to reformulate his ideas about the way the evolutionary development of man has proceeded: "Man had not remained one species, but had differentiated into two distinct animals." He has to modify his previous "Darwinian" explanation by a "Marxist" one: "it seemed clear as daylight to me that the gradual widening of the merely temporary and social difference between the Capitalist and the Labourer was the key to the whole position." Even in his own day, he reflects, men tend to spend more and more time underground: "There is a tendency to utilise underground space for the less ornamental purposes of civilisation." Even now, does not an East-end worker live in such artificial conditions as practically to be cut off from the natural surface of the earth?" Similarly the rich have tended to preserve themselves more and more as an exclusive and self-contained group, with fewer and fewer social contacts with the workers, until society has stratified rigidly into a two-class system. "So, in the end, above ground, you must have the Haves, pursuing pleasure and comfort and beauty, and below ground the Have-nots; the workers getting continually adapted to the conditions of their labour." The analysis represents, it will be seen, a romantic and pessimistic variant of orthodox Marxist thought: the implications of the class-war are accepted, but the possibility of the successful proletarian revolution establishing a classless society is rigidly excluded. Thus, the traveller concludes, the social tendencies of nineteenth century industrialism have become rigidified and then built in, as it were, to the evolutionary development of the race. Nevertheless, he is still orthodox enough in his analysis to assume that the Eloi, despite their physical and mental decline, are still the masters and the Morlocks—as he finds the underground creatures are called—are their slaves. It is not long before he discovers that this, too, is a false conclusion.

Soon enough, despite his dalliance with Weena, and her obvious reluctance to let him go, the traveller decides that he must find out more about the Morlocks, and resolves to descend into their underworld. It is at this point that, in Pritchett's phrase, "the story alters its key, and the Time Traveller reveals the foundation of slime and horror on which the pretty life of his Arcadians is precariously and fearfully resting." [4] The descent of the traveller into the underworld has, in fact, an almost undisplaced mythical significance: it suggests a parody of the Harrowing of Hell, where it is not the souls of the just that are released but the demonic Morlocks, for it is they who dominate the subsequent narrative. During his "descent into hell" the traveller is seized by the Morlocks, but he keeps them at bay by striking matches, for they recoil from light in any form, which is why they do not normally appear on the surface of the earth by day. During his brief and confused visit to their world he sees and hears great machines at work, and notices a table spread for a meal. He observes that the Morlocks are carnivorous, but does not, for a time, draw the obvious conclusion about the nature of the meat they are eating. However, it is readily apparent to the reader. The Morlocks have a complex symbolic function, for they not only represent an exaggerated fear of the nineteenth century proletariat, but also embody many of the traditional mythical images of a demonic world. This will soon be apparent if one compares Wells's account of them and their environment with the chapter on "Demonic Imagery" in Northrop Frye's *Anatomy of Criticism*. As Frye writes:

> Images of perverted work belong here too: engines of torture, weapons of war, armour, and images of a dead mechanism which, because it does not humanise nature, is unnatural as well as inhuman. Corresponding to the temple or One Building of the Apocalypse, we have the prison or dungeon, the sealed furnace of heat without light, like the city of Dis in Dante. [5]

[4] ["The Scientific Romances" in *The Living Novel*. It is the essay preceding this in the present volume.—Ed.]

[5] *Anatomy of Criticism*, p. 150.

Indeed nothing is more remarkable about *The Time Machine* than the way in which its central narrative is polarised between opposed groups of imagery, the paradisal (or, in Frye's phrase, the apocalyptic) and the demonic, representing extreme forms of human desire and repulsion.

A further significance of the Morlocks can be seen in the fact that they are frequently referred to in terms of unpleasant animal life: thus they are described as, or compared with, "apes," "lemurs," "worms," "spiders," and "rats." One must compare these images with the traveller's original discovery that all forms of non-human animal life—with the apparent exception of butterflies—had been banished from the upper world, whether noxious or not. There is a powerful irony in his subsequent discovery that the one remaining form of animal life, and the most noxious of all, is a branch of humanity. Furthermore this confusion of human and animal—with its origin in some kind of imaginative perturbation over the deeper implications of Darwinism—was to provide the central theme of *The Island of Dr. Moreau.*

The traveller narrowly escapes with his life from the Morlocks and returns to the surface to make another reappraisal of the world of 802701. The image of the "golden age" as it has presented itself to him on his arrival has been destroyed: "there was an altogether new element in the sickening quality of the Morlocks—a something inhuman and malign." He has to reject his subsequent hypothesis that the Eloi were the masters, and the Morlocks their slaves. A new relationship has clearly evolved between the two races; the Eloi, who are in terror of dark and moonless nights, are in some way victims of the Morlocks, though he is still not certain precisely how. His experience underground has shattered his previous euphoria (symbolically perhaps an end of the paradisal innocence in which he has been participating), and his natural inventiveness and curiosity reassert themselves. He makes his way with Weena to a large green building that he has seen in the distance many miles off, which he later calls "the Palace of Green Porcelain." On their way they spend a night in the open: the traveller looks at the stars in their now unfamiliar arrangements and reflects on his present isolation.

> Looking at these stars suddenly dwarfed my own troubles and all the gravities of terrestrial life. I thought of their unfathomable

distance and the slow inevitable drift of their movements out of
the unknown past into the unknown future. I thought of the great
precessional cycle that the pole of the earth describes. Only forty
times had that silent revolution occurred during all the years that
I had traversed. And during these few revolutions all the activity,
all the traditions, the complex organisations, the nations, languages, literatures, aspirations, even the mere memory of Man as
I knew him, had been swept out of existence. Instead were these
frail creatures who had forgotten their high ancestry, and the
white Things of which I went in terror. Then I thought of the
Great Fear that was between the two species, and for the first
time, with a sudden shiver, came the clear knowledge of what the
meat I had seen might be. Yet it was too horrible! I looked at
little Weena sleeping beside me, her face white and star-like
under the stars, and forthwith dismissed the thought.

The traveller's knowledge of the world of the Eloi and the
Morlocks, and the relation between them, is almost complete.
When they reach the Palace of Green Porcelain, he finds, as if to
belie his reflections on the disappearance of all traces of the past,
that it is a vast museum: "Clearly we stood among the ruins of
some latter-day South Kensington!" The museum, with its
semi-ruinous remains of earlier phases of human achievement,
puts the traveller once more in a direct emotional relation with
the past, and, by implication, with his own age. Here, the
Arcadian spell is finally cast off. He remembers that he is, after
all, a late-Victorian scientist with a keen interest in technology.
He is intrigued by various great machines, some half destroyed,
and others in quite good condition:

> You know I have a certain weakness for mechanism, and I was
> inclined to linger among these: the more so as for the most part
> they had the interest of puzzles, and I could make only the
> vaguest guesses at what they were for. I fancied that if I could
> solve their puzzles I should find myself in possession of powers that
> might be of use against the Morlocks.

The Morlocks, after all, are a technological race, and if he is to
defend himself against them—as he has decided he must—he
must match himself against their mechanical prowess. The
images of machinery in this part of the narrative are sufficient to
suggest to the reader the presence of the Morlocks, and before
long the traveller sees footprints in the dust around him, and

hears noises coming from one end of a long gallery, which mean that the Morlocks are not far away. He breaks an iron lever off one of the machines to use as a mace. By now, his feelings for the Morlocks are those of passionate loathing: "I longed very much to kill a Morlock or so. Very inhuman, you may think, to want to go killing one's own descendants! But it was impossible, some-how, to feel any humanity in the things." Since the Morlocks on one level stand for the late nineteenth century proletariat, the traveller's attitude towards them clearly symbolises a contempo-rary bourgeois fear of the working class, and it is not fanciful to impute something of this attitude to Wells himself. From his schooldays in Bromley he had disliked and feared the working class in a way wholly appropriate to the son of a small tradesman—as various Marxist critics have not been slow to remark. The traveller's gradual identification with the beautiful and aristocratic—if decadent—Eloi against the brutish Morlocks is indicative of Wells's own attitudes, or one aspect of them, and links up with a common theme in his realistic fiction: the hypergamous aspirations of a low-born hero towards genteel heroines: Jessica Milton in *The Wheels of Chance*, Helen Walsing-ham in *Kipps*, Beatrice Normandy in *Tono-Bungay*, and Christabel in *Mr. Polly*.

Wells's imagination was easily given to producing images of mutilation and violence, and the traveller's hatred of the Morlocks gives them free rein. The reader is further prepared for the scenes of violence and destruction which end the traveller's expedition to the museum by his discovery of "a long gallery of rusting stands of arms," where he "hesitated between my crowbar and a hatchet or a sword." But he could not carry both and kept the crowbar. He contented himself with a jar of camphor from another part of the museum, since this was inflammable and would make a useful weapon against the Morlocks. By now we have wholly moved from the dominantly paradisal imagery of the first half of the narrative to the demonic imagery of the second. Instead of a golden age, or lotos land, we are back in the familiar world of inventiveness and struggle.

When Weena and the traveller are once more outside the mu-seum and are making their way homeward through the woods, he decides to keep the lurking Morlocks at bay during the coming night by lighting a fire. He succeeds only too well, and before long discovers that he has set the whole forest ablaze. Several Morlocks try to attack him, but he fights them off with his iron bar. He then discovers the creatures all fleeing in panic before the advancing fire: in the confusion Weena is lost. There are some powerful descriptions of the Morlocks' plight:

> And now I was to see the most weird and horrible thing, I think, of all that I beheld in that future age. This whole space was as bright as day with the reflection of the fire. In the centre was a hillock or tumulus, surmounted by a scorched hawthorn. Beyond this was another arm of the burning forest, with yellow tongues already writhing from it, completely encircling the space with a fence of fire. Upon the hillside were some thirty or forty Morlocks, dazzled by the light and heat and blundering hither and thither against each other in their bewilderment. At first I did not realise their blindness, and struck furiously at them with my bar, in a frenzy of fear, as they approached me, killing one and crippling several more. But when I watched the gestures of one of them groping under the hawthorn against the red sky, and heard their moans, I was assured of their absolute helplessness and misery in the glare, and I struck no more of them.

Eventually, on the following morning, the traveller gets back to the neighbourhood of the White Sphinx, whence he had started. Everything is as it was when he left. The beautiful Eloi are still moving across the landscape in their gay robes, or bathing in the river. But now his disillusion with their Arcadian world and his realisation of the true nature of their lives is complete.

> I understood now what all the beauty of the over-world people covered. Very pleasant was their day, as pleasant as the day of the cattle in the field. Like the cattle they knew of no enemies, and provided against no needs. And their end was the same.

Here we have the solution to a riddle that was implicitly posed at the beginning of the traveller's narrative. Soon after his arrival among the Eloi he had found that there were no domestic animals in their world: "horses, cattle, sheep, dogs, had followed the Ichthyosaurus into extinction." Yet the life led by the Eloi is clearly that contained in conventional literary pastoral, and the first part of the traveller's narrative partakes of the nature of pastoral—but it is a pastoral world without sheep or cattle. And a little later, during his speculations on the possibilities of eugenic development, he had reflected:

> We improve our favourite plants and animals—and how few they
> are—gradually by selective breeding; now a new and better
> peach, now a seedless grape, now a sweeter and larger flower, now
> a more convenient breed of cattle.

Something of the sort, he concludes, has brought about the world
of 802701. But the paradox latent in the observation is only made
manifest in his return from the museum, now possessing a
complete knowledge of this world. There are no sheep or cattle in
the pastoral world of the Eloi because they are themselves the
cattle, fattened and fed by their underground masters. They are
both a "sweeter and larger flower" and "a more convenient breed
of cattle." Thus the complex symbolism of the central narrative
of *The Time Machine* is ingeniously completed on this note of
diabolical irony. Such knowledge has made the Arcadian world
intolerable to the traveller. He is now able to escape from it: the
Morlocks have produced his machine and placed it as a trap for
him, but he is able to elude them, and travels off into the still
more remote future.

The final part of the time traveller's narrative, the chapter
called "The Further Vision," is an extended epilogue to the story
of the Eloi and the Morlocks. The traveller moves further and
further into the future, until he reaches an age when all traces of
humanity have vanished and the world is given over to giant
crabs. The earth has ceased to rotate, and has come to rest with
one face always turned to the sun:

> I stopped very gently and sat upon the Time Machine, looking
> round. The sky was no longer blue. North-eastward it was inky
> black, and out of the darkness shone brightly and steadily the pale
> white stars. Overhead it was a deep Indian red and starless, and
> south-eastward it grew brighter to a growing scarlet where, cut by
> the horizon, lay the huge hull of the sun, red and motionless. The
> rocks about me were of a harsh, reddish colour, and all the trace
> of life that I could see at first was the intensely green vegetation
> that covered every projecting point on their south-eastern face. It
> was the same rich green that one sees on forest moss or on lichen
> in caves: plants which like these grow in a perpetual twilight.

The whole of this vision of a dying world is conveyed with a
poetic intensity which Wells was never to recapture. The
transition from the social and biological interest of the "802701"

episode to the cosmological note of these final pages is extremely
well done: the previous account of the decline of humanity is
echoed and amplified by the description of the gradual death of
the whole physical world. The traveller moves on and on, seeking
to discover the ultimate mystery of the world's fate.

> At last, more than thirty million years hence, the huge red-hot
> dome of the sun had come to obscure nearly a tenth part of the
> darkling heavens. Then I stopped once more, for the crawling
> multitude of crabs had disappeared, and the red beach, save for
> its livid green liverworts and lichens, seemed lifeless. And now it
> was flecked with white. A bitter cold assailed me. Rare white
> flakes ever and again came eddying down. To the north-eastward,
> the glare of snow lay under the starlight of the sable sky, and I
> could see an undulating crest of hillocks pinkish-white. There
> were fringes of ice along the sea margin, with drifting masses
> further out; but the main expanse of that salt ocean, all bloody
> under the eternal sunset, was still unfrozen.

Finally, after an eclipse of the sun has reduced this desolate
world to total darkness, the traveller returns to his own time, and
the waiting circle of friends in his house at Richmond.

A contemporary reviewer paid special tribute to these final
pages, and referred to "that last *fin de siècle,* when earth is
moribund and man has ceased to be." [6] This reference to the *fin
de siècle* is appropriate both in its immediate context and in a
larger sense, for, as I have already suggested, *The Time Machine* is
pre-eminently a book of its time, giving imaginative form to
many of the fears and preoccupations of the final years of the
nineteenth century. Max Nordau, in fact, had attacked these
preoccupations and attitudes in a passage which curiously
anticipates the themes and dominant images of *The Time Machine*:

> *Fin de siècle* is at once a confession and a complaint. The old
> Northern faith contained the fearsome doctrine of the Dusk of the
> Gods. In our days there have arisen in more highly developed
> minds vague qualms of a Dusk of the Nations, in which all suns
> and all stars are gradually waning, and mankind with all its
> institutions and creations is perishing in the midst of a dying
> world. [7]

[6] *Daily Chronicle*, 27 July, 1895.
[7] *Degeneration* (London, 1895), p. 2.

Since *The Time Machine* is a romance and not a piece of realistic fiction, it conveys its meaning in poetic fashion through images, rather than by the revelation of character in action. It is, in short, a myth, and in Shanks's words, "can be interpreted in many ways, none of them quite consistent, all of them more alive and fruitful than the rigid allegorical correspondence." I have tried to indicate some of the thematic strands to be found in the work. Some of them are peculiarly of their period, others have a more general and a more fundamental human relevance. The opposition of Eloi and Morlocks can be interpreted in terms of the late nineteenth-century class struggle, but it also reflects an opposition between aestheticism and utilitarianism, pastoralism and technology, contemplation and action, and ultimately, and least specifically, between beauty and ugliness, and light and darkness. The book not only embodies the tensions and dilemmas of its time, but others peculiar to Wells himself, which a few years later were to make him cease to be an artist, and become a propagandist. Since the tensions are imaginatively and not intellectually resolved we find that a note of irony becomes increasingly more pronounced as the traveller persists in his disconcerting exploration of the world where he has found himself. *The Time Machine* is not only a myth, but an ironic myth, like many other considerable works of modern literature. And despite the complexity of its thematic elements, Wells's art is such that the story is a skilfully wrought imaginative whole, a single image.

The Logic of "Prophecy"
in *The Time Machine*

by Robert M. Philmus

The statements that H. G. Wells gave out in the twenties and thirties about his early "scientific romances" or "scientific fantasies," as he alternately called them, are not sympathetic to the spirit of these works, the best of which he had written before the turn of the century. In general, he makes them out to be slighter in substance or more tendentious in tone than the serious reader coming upon them now is prepared to find them. But unlike a number of other modern writers who have commented on the meaning of their works, Wells does not attempt wilfully to mislead or mystify his readers; and in fact his own criticism of his fiction is sometimes actively helpful in dealing with it.

Of particular importance are his various observations about *The Time Machine*; and his preface to the *Scientific Romances* especially—an indispensable account of the theory and practice of his science fiction—draws attention to two aspects of his first book-length "scientific romance" essential to its interpretation. The first point concerns the Time Traveller's vision of the future, a vision Wells characterizes as running "counter to the placid assumption of that time that Evolution was a pro-human force making things better and better for mankind." The second point, already implicit in this last remark from the preface, is that *The Time Machine* is an "assault on human self-satisfaction." [1]

Despite the absence of detail and specificity in these statements

"The Logic of 'Prophecy' in *The Time Machine*" by Robert M. Philmus. Originally published as "*The Time Machine*; or, the Fourth Dimension as Prophecy" in *PMLA* 84 (1969), pp. 530–35. This revised version is reprinted by permission of the Modern Language Association of America and the author.

[1] *The Scientific Romances of H. G. Wells* (London, 1933), p. ix.

of Wells's, they in effect anticipate and summarize subsequent studies of *The Time Machine* as an "ironic myth" of degeneration and as "a serious attack on human complacency." [2] What remains unexplained, however, is the Traveller's compulsion to resume his time-travelling—to return, perhaps, to the world of the Eloi and the Morlocks; and it is towards an explanation of this response to the "vision," or "prophecy," of *The Time Machine* that my own interpretation is directed. To arrive at an explanation, I propose heuristically to resolve *The Time Machine* into its several component parts and to examine each of them in itself and in relation to the rest; namely, the Time Traveller's vision of the future, his understanding of that vision, and the reaction of the fictive audience to his prophetic report.[3]

I

Concerning *The Time Machine*'s vision of the future, "degeneration" is not, it seems to me, a precise enough description of the backsliding of the human species into the less and less recognizably anthropomorphic descendants that the Time Traveller finds in the world of 802,701 and beyond. It is true that Wells used that term himself as early as 1891 in an essay which outlines abstractly the idea behind this vision of the future.[4] But in that

[2] The first of these two views is that of Bernard Bergonzi in "*The Time Machine*: An Ironic Myth," *Critical Quarterly*, II (1960), 293–305, and *The Early H. G. Wells: A Study of the Scientific Romances* (Toronto, 1961), pp. 3–14, 42–61 *passim;* the second belongs to Mark R. Hillegas, "Cosmic Pessimism in H. G. Wells's Scientific Romances," *Papers of the Michigan Academy of Science, Art and Letters*, XLVI (1961), 657–658, and *The Future as Nightmare: H. G. Wells and the Anti-Utopians* (New York, 1967), pp. 24–34 *passim.*

[3] All published drafts of *The Time Machine* share these components, though the serialized versions appearing in the *National Observer* and the *New Review* differ from the (subsequent) first English edition, published by Heinemann, in many respects—not all of them minor. While I cite passages from the serial versions as outside evidence for my interpretation of the (Heinemann) *Time Machine*, no attempt is made here to examine the differences among the various published versions as regards their meaning or literary merit. David Y. Hughes and I have undertaken such an exploration in Chapter 3 of *H. G. Wells: Early Writings in Science and Science Fiction* (Berkeley, 1974); see also Bergonzi, "The Publication of *The Time Machine*, 1894–5," *Review of English Studies*, n.s. IX (1960), 42–51.

[4] That Wells was familiar with the notion of degeneration this early seems to me to reduce greatly the possible extent of any influence on him of Max

same essay, entitled "Zoological Retrogression," he also calls this
process of reversion "degradation," [5] which suggests the step-by-
step decline from man to beast that he was to take up in *The
Island of Doctor Moreau* (1896) as well. More accurately still, the
gradual reduction of homo sapiens to—or his replacement
by—species lower and lower on the evolutionary scale can be
seen as a vision of "devolution"—that is, evolution in reverse.

Beginning in light among the "childlike" Eloi (p. 38)[6]—for a
while supposed to be the sole degraded species inhabiting the
"Golden Age" of 802,701—the Time Traveller's narrative moves
inevitably towards the impending darkness which fearfully
attracts him: first "the darkness of the new moon" (p. 96) and
later, in a chapter called "The Further Vision," the total
blackness of the solar eclipse. The oppressive, almost manichean,
threat to the paradisal "upper-world" of the Eloi which the dark
and demonic "under-world" of the Morlocks imposes[7] is something which the Time Traveller cannot forget once he has
become aware of it. Though in escaping from this world where
humanity has devolved and bifurcated into the "ape-like" and
predatory Morlocks (p. 79) and the feeble and preyed upon Eloi
he recalls that "The darkness presently fell from my eyes" (p.
133), he soon has occasion to perceive that the forces of darkness
threaten to extinguish the world of sunlight completely. The
Morlocks embody a "modification of the human type . . . far
more profound than among the 'Eloi' " (p. 85); but, as the
Traveller soon discovers, the process of devolution has by no
means reached an equilibrium.

The paradise-hell of the Eloi and the Morlocks prepares
for—and perhaps, in biological terms, leads to—what the
Traveller sees as the further vision of devolution—devolution
tending ultimately towards the extinction of all life. In an episode
appearing in the *New Review* but deleted subsequently, he comes

---

Nordau's *Degeneration* (1894), adduced by Bergonzi (in *The Early H. G. Wells*) as
a possible source for the vision of the future in *The Time Machine*.

[5] "Zoological Retrogression," *The Gentleman's Magazine*, CCLXXI (Sept.,
1891), p. 246.

[6] All quotations from *The Time Machine* refer to the Heinemann edition
(London, 1895).

[7] As Bergonzi observes of *The Time Machine*, "its central narrative is polarised
between opposed groups of imagery, the paradisal . . . and the demonic" ("An
Ironic Myth," p. 300).

next upon a species more degraded than the Morlocks. Of this
creature, which he likens to "rabbits or some breed of kangaroo,"
the Traveller reports: "I was surprised to see that the thing had
five feeble digits to both its fore and hind feet—the fore feet,
indeed, were almost as human as the fore feet of a frog. It had,
moreover, a roundish head, with a projecting forehead and
forward-looking eyes." He admits that as a result of his
examination, "A disagreeable apprehension crossed my mind";
and though he does not say explicitly what this apprehension is,
he does mention that his being stalked by a monster similar to a
gigantic centipede forced him to leave "my grey animal, or grey
man, whichever it was." [8] It is left for the reader to infer that at
this point in the future the hominid-derived Eloi or Morlocks
have devolved into creatures with "five feeble digits" which are
now the victims of giant centipedes.[9]

At the next stop in the distant future (in both the Heinemann
and the *New Review* versions) anything even remotely resembling
anthropomorphic life seems to have disappeared, and the
Traveller sees instead "a thing like a huge white butterfly" and

[8] "The Further Vision," *New Review*, XII (1895), 578–579. Wells probably
added the incident with the "grey animal, or grey man" because W. E. Henley,
the new editor of the *Review*, told him he needed more copy (see Bergonzi, "The
Publication," pp. 44–45).

[9] The origin of these giant centipedes is open to conjecture. They may derive
from some "humble creature" unnoticed in the world of the Eloi and the
Morlocks (see the quotation from "Zoological Retrogression" below); or—as a
period of unspecified scope is being compressed (i.e., the temporal "distance"
between this point and 802,701)—their ancestors may be the Eloi or Morlocks
themselves. The lack of any overt resemblance between the latter two species
and the "centipedes" does not conclusively discount this last possibility: in
"Zoological Retrogression" Wells telescopes evolutionary time in making homo
sapiens a member of "the mud-fish family" and in the process calls attention to
the paradoxical dissimilarity between man and mud-fish. Thus it is not
impossible that the prey (the Eloi) have been transformed through degenerative
adaptation into predators (the "centipedes")—which would be the kind of
"poetic justice" manifesting itself when man "goes down to the sea in ships, and
with wide-sweeping nets and hooks cunningly baited, beguiles the children of
those who drove his ancestors out of the water" ("Retrogression," p. 253). And
it is equally possible that the structural relationship of predator and prey
maintains itself: the Eloi may, through natural selection, become degraded to
"rabbits or some breed of kangaroo," finally to "a thing like a huge white
butterfly," while the Morlocks retain their predator status as giant centipedes
and later monstrous crab-like creatures. The one thing that is certain is the
devolutionary pattern implicit in these transformations.

"a monstrous crab-like creature" (p. 137). He goes on until, thirty million years hence, it *appears* as if animal life has devolved out of existence. Plant life has degenerated to "livid green liverworts and lichens" (p. 139). Here he witnesses a solar eclipse which prefigures the end of the world.

> The darkness grew apace; a cold wind began to blow in freshening gusts from the east, and the showering white flakes in the air increased in number. From the edge of the sea came a ripple and a whisper. Beyond these lifeless sounds the world was silent. Silent? It would be hard to convey the stillness of it . . . As the darkness thickened, the eddying flakes grew more abundant . . . and the cold of the air more intense. At last, one by one, swiftly, one after the other, the white peaks of the distant hills vanished into blackness. The breeze rose to a moaning wind. I saw the black central shadow of the eclipse sweeping towards me. In another moment the pale stars alone were visible. All else was rayless obscurity. The sky was absolutely black. (pp. 140–141)

In retrospect, it seems that the unbalanced struggle between the Eloi and the Morlocks prepares for this final vision, that a terrible logic compels the conclusion: "The sky was absolutely black." "People unfamiliar with such speculations as those of the younger Darwin," the Time Traveller had remarked earlier, "forget that the planets must ultimately fall back into the parent body" (p. 76). This is a vision hardly in accord with "Excelsior" optimism, however much the notion of falling "back into the parent body" anticipates the Freudian formulation of the "death wish." On the contrary, the allusion to G. H. Darwin's Theory of Tidal Evolution reinforces, on a more cosmic scale, *The Time Machine*'s vision of life retracing its evolutionary path back to the sea and thence, it may be presumed, out of existence.

This vision, precisely calculated to "run counter to the placid assumption . . . that Evolution was a pro-human force making things better and better for mankind," dramatizes an idea that Wells, in "Zoological Retrogression," calls an "evolutionary antithesis":

> . . . there is almost always associated with the suggestion of advance in biological phenomena an opposite idea, which is its essential complement. The technicality expressing this would, if it obtained sufficient currency in the world of culture, do much to reconcile the naturalist and his traducers. The toneless glare of

> optimistic evolution would then be softened by a shadow; the monstrous reiteration of "Excelsior" by people who did not climb would cease; the too sweet harmony of the spheres would be enhanced by a discord, this evolutionary antithesis—degradation. ("Zoological Retrogression," p. 246)

Wells goes on to illustrate "the enormous importance of degeneration as a plastic process in nature" and its "parity with evolution" (p. 246) by giving examples of species which have retrogressed to survive (hence "plastic process") and of vestigial features now observable which perhaps presage future degeneration. He focuses particularly upon the mud-fish, ancestor of all the land animals—a creature which fled from the sea, where it was outmatched in the struggle for existence, and retrogressively adapted itself to existence on land (pp. 251–252). His concluding remarks on the fate that may be in store for "the last of the mud-fish family, man," are especially relevant to the vision of the future in *The Time Machine*.

> There is . . . no guarantee [writes Wells] in scientific knowledge of man's permanence or permanent ascendancy . . . The presumption is that before him lies a long future of profound modification, but whether this will be, according to his present ideals, upward or downward, no one can forecast. Still, so far as any scientist can tell us, it may be that, instead of this, Nature is, in unsuspected obscurity, equipping some now humble creature with wider possibilities of appetite, endurance, or destruction, to rise in the fulness of time and sweep *homo* away into the darkness from which his universe arose. The Coming Beast must certainly be reckoned in any anticipatory calculations regarding the Coming Man. ("Zoological Retrogression," p. 253)[10]

Clearly Wells's speculation here goes well beyond the mere softening of the "glare of optimistic evolution" with a "shadow." Indeed, he is fascinated by this "opposite idea": the vision of man's being swept away "into the darkness from which his universe arose"—of "life that . . . is slowly and remorselessly annihilated," as he says in "On Extinction"[11]—the vision, in other words, of *The Time Machine*. His "Coming Beast" is more

---

[10] For a fuller discussion of this "opposite idea" and the apocalyptic biology behind it, see Philmus and Hughes, *H. G. Wells (op. cit.)*, Chapter 5.

[11] "On Extinction," *Chambers's Journal*, X (Sept. 30, 1893), 623.

literal than Yeats's in "The Second Coming" (1920) and
dominates stories like "The Sea Raiders" (1896), *The War of the
Worlds* (1898), and "The Empire of the Ants" (1904) as well as
The Time Machine.

II

The vision of the future as a devolutionary process, reversing as
it does the expectations of "optimistic evolution," is not isolated
in *The Time Machine* as an imaginative possibility exploited for its
own sake. The structure of the world of the Eloi and the
Morlocks, for instance, suggests a critique of the pastoral utopia
of *News from Nowhere* (1890) and other pre-Wellsian utopian
fiction, since the idyllic world of the Eloi is quite literally
undermined by industrial technology. Such a critique is relevant
to an understanding of that point of view in *The Time Machine*
which comprehends the reactions of both the Time Traveller and
his audience to this vision of the future. To locate this point of
view, however, it is first necessary to assess the significance of the
Traveller's theories about the world of 802,701—theories which
mediate between future and present.

Although the Traveller refines and somewhat revises his
hypothesis as he learns more about the nature of the Morlocks,
he temporarily settles on an etiological interpretation of the
relationship between these fairly energetic predators and their
effete and virtually androgynous victims.

> The great triumph of Humanity I had dreamed of took a
> different shape in my mind. It had been no such triumph of moral
> education and general co-operation as I had imagined. Instead, I
> saw a real aristocracy, armed with perfected science and working
> to a logical conclusion the industrial system of to-day. Its triumph
> had not been simply a triumph over nature, but a triumph over
> nature and the fellow-man. (p. 84)

To be sure, he himself reserves a doubt concerning his account of
how this future world had come to be: "My explanation may be
absolutely wrong. I still think it is the most plausible one." But
his ambivalence here reminds one, not accidentally, of his
subsequent remark as to how the reader may accept this vision:

"Take it as a lie—or a prophecy . . . Consider I have been speculating on the destinies of our race, until I have hatched this fiction" (p. 145). Together these statements on the part of the Time Traveller suggest that any explanation of the imaginary world of the Eloi and the Morlocks is admissible only insofar as it recognizes the future projected in the fiction as "prophecy"— that is, the "working to a logical conclusion" of what can be observed in the world of the present.

The Time Traveller's various hypotheses are all of them "prophetic" in that sense. He arrives at them by extrapolating from tendencies existing in the present, as he explicitly states in saying:

> At first, *proceeding from the problems of our own age,* it seemed clear as daylight to me that the gradual widening of the present merely temporary and social difference between the Capitalist and the Labourer, was the key to the whole position. No doubt it will seem grotesque enough to you—and wildly incredible!—and yet even now there are circumstances to point that way. (p. 82; emphasis added)

The implication here is that the procedure for interpreting the vision of *The Time Machine* recapitulates the process by which the fiction was "hatched"; so that the science-fictional method of "prophecy" is itself "the key to the whole position." Looked at in this way, the "prophecy" can be seen to embody the consequences not, precisely speaking, of "the industrial system of to-day" but of the ideal directing the course and uses of technological advance.

An indictment of man's "present ideals" emerges from the Time Traveller's hypotheses in their evaluative—as distinguishable from their descriptive—aspect. In saying, for example, that "the great triumph of Humanity . . . had not been simply a triumph over nature" (as T. H. Huxley had urged)[12] "but a triumph over nature and the fellow-man," the Time Traveller intimates a negative moral judgment, a failure of "moral education and general co-operation." And condemnation is again involved in his observation that human intellect "had set

---

[12] In "Evolution and Ethics" and other essays, Huxley declares that ethical man can exist only if he modifies the "cosmic process."

itself steadfastly towards comfort and ease, a balanced society with security as its watchword"—since "Only those animals partake of intelligence that have to meet a huge variety of needs and dangers" (p. 130). The ideal (perfect security) therefore undermines the means of maintaining it (intelligence); and the result, the Traveller insists, is that "the upper-world man had drifted towards his feeble prettiness, and the under-world to mere mechanical industry. But that perfect state had lacked one thing even for mechanical perfection—absolute permanency" (pp. 130–131). This final interpretation, which elaborates upon and at the same time supersedes his earlier explanation, accounts more fully for the world of the Eloi and the Morlocks as it obviously impugns man's "present ideals." The ideal of subjugating "nature and the fellow-man" to bring about a state of "comfort and ease" is evaluated—and satirized—by projecting its consequences as a vision of the future.

Both the Traveller's method of interpreting the vision and the process by which that vision was "hatched" assume, therefore, that man's ideals do affect the course of evolution, that the world of 802,701 and beyond is the "working to a logical conclusion" of man's striving for comfort and ease. This point is most unmistakable in the version of *The Time Machine* serialized by the *National Observer*. In an episode called "The Refinement of Humanity: A.D. 12,203," the Philosophical Inventor (as Wells initially styled the Time Traveller) rebukes a doctor in his audience:

> You believe that the average height, average weight, average longevity will all be increased, that in the future humanity will breed and sanitate itself into human Megatheria . . . But . . . what I saw is just what one might have expected. Man, like other animals, has been moulded, and will be, by the necessities of his environment. What keeps men so large and strong as they are? The fact that if any drop below a certain level of power and capacity for competition, they die. Remove dangers, render physical exertion no longer a necessity but an excrescence upon life, abolish competition by limiting population . . . [and degeneration results]
>
> Somewhere between now and then [i.e., 12,203] your sanitary science must have won the battle it is beginning now.[13]

[13] "The Refinement of Humanity," *National Observer*, n.s. XI (Apr. 24, 1894), 581–582.

The causal connection Wells makes between degeneration and "sanitary science" here helps to clarify how, in subsequent versions of *The Time Machine*, a vision antithetical to "the placid assumption . . . that Evolution was a pro-human force" can also illustrate the consequences of an ideal seemingly inseparable from that assumption—namely, the ideal of evolving towards greater and greater "comfort and ease."

In terms of the Time Traveller's theories, then, it can be said that the "horrible degeneration [of homo sapiens] has occurred because mankind, as Huxley feared, was *ultimately* unable to control the cosmic or evolutionary process. [14] That is, mankind, the Traveller implies, apparently controlled the cosmic process too well, according to an ideal the consequences of which no one could foresee. One of those consequences is that by 802,701 no species has sufficient intelligence to set limits on the struggle for existence, in which the defenseless Eloi fall victims to the carnivorous Morlocks. Among these descendants of homo sapiens, the struggle for survival—which, engendered by "Necessity," makes the "absolute permanency" of "mechanical perfection" impossible—now resumes the character that struggle takes among other animals. "Man," the Time Traveller reflects, "had been content to live in ease and delight upon the labours of his fellow-man, had taken Necessity as his watchword and excuse, and in the fulness of time Necessity had come home to him" (pp. 105–106). And once Darwinian "Necessity" reasserts itself, once, that is to say, the pressures of natural selection cause homo sapiens to begin reverting to beasts, anthropomorphic life is irrevocably on the downward path of devolution, whose "logical conclusion" is extinction.

III

The vision of social disintegration and devolution as a critique of the present ideal of striving towards "ease and delight" can exist only in the dimension of "prophecy," that dimension into which the critique can be projected and imaginatively given life—the world, in other words, of science fiction. [15] The "Fourth

[14] Hillegas, "Cosmic Pessimism," p. 658; emphasis added.
[15] As late as *Men like Gods* (1923), the utopian fantasy which takes place in the

Dimension" as a time dimension is thus a kind of metaphor: it is
the dimension open to the imagination. "Our mental existences,
which are immaterial and have no dimensions, are passing along
the Time-Dimension" (p. 6), the Traveller had said in introduc-
ing his audience to the concept of this new dimension. As a place
where the consequences of accepted ideals can be envisioned, the
Fourth Dimension provides a critical and comprehensive point of
view from which to survey and evaluate the present.

That at the outset no one except the Time Traveller has
conceived of—or even can conceive of—this dimension already
indicates a lack of imaginative (and critical) awareness on the
part of his fictive audience. His argument for a Fourth Dimension, prefaced by the caveat that "I shall have to controvert one
or two ideas that are almost universally accepted" (pp. 1–2),
meets with incomprehension and complacent skepticism. Quite
predictably, his audience fails to take seriously—if the point is
grasped at all—the relevance of the Time Traveller's vision.
None of his auditors seems to connect the vision of "The two
species that had resulted from the evolution of man . . . sliding
down towards, or . . . already arrived at, an altogether new
relationship" (p. 97) with his own preconception of an "inevitable tendency to higher and better things" ("Retrogression," p.
247). Perhaps no one in the audience takes this vision seriously
because, as Wells surmised elsewhere, "It is part of the excessive
egotism of the human animal that the bare idea of its extinction
seems incredible to it." [16] Certainly there is no sign that anyone
among the listeners sees how, or that, the Time Traveller's vision
implicates his "present ideals," which are responsible for the
shape of the future. On the contrary, the reactions which typify
the attitude of the audience are the skepticism of the Medical
Man, who wants to analyze the flowers the Traveller has brought
back with him, and the arrant disbelief of the Editor, who thinks
the whole business a "gaudy lie" (p. 148). Only the unidentified

---

"F dimension," Wells has one of his characters say of another (neither has yet
entered the utopia): "He has always had too much imagination. He thinks that
things that don't exist *can* exist. And now he imagines himself in some sort of
scientific romance and out of our world altogether" (*Men like Gods* [New York,
1923], pp. 21–22).

[16] "The Extinction of Man," *Certain Personal Matters* (London, 1898 [1897]), p.
172. This is a slightly altered version of an essay first appearing in the *Pall Mall
Gazette* for Sept. 23, 1894.

narrator of the entire *Time Machine* stays "awake most of the night thinking about it" (p. 148).

In fact, the Time Traveller himself does not seem to be wholly cognizant of the implications of his theories. If his etiology is correct, then the cause of the degeneration he discovers exists in the present. Therefore, the burden of what he calls "moral education" remains here and now; and his return into the Fourth Dimension—perhaps back to 802,701—would appear to be either a romantic evasion of a piece with his sentimental "squirms of idyllic petting" that V. S. Pritchett finds embarrassing,[17] or a pessimistic retreat from a world "that must inevitably fall back upon and destroy its makers" (p. 152). In any case, the Time Traveller's point of view, though more comprehensive than that of any of the other characters, is still limited; and this limitation finds its structural correlative in the fact that his narrative is related secondhand, as it were, three years after his disappearance, and comprises only a part—albeit a large part—of the fiction.

That the structure of *The Time Machine* encompasses, and thereby defines the limits of, the Traveller's point of view[18] indicates that the romance follows an inner logic of its own, a logic, like that governing the Time Traveller's vision, which compels ultimate consequences from a given premise. Accordingly, the logic that necessitates the Traveller's vanishing into the world of his vision derives from how he accepts that vision. His insistence that "The story I told you was true" (p. 148) suggests that he takes his vision literally, that he allows it the same ontological status that he himself has. Hence to dramatize the assertion that he has told the literal truth, he must go back into the Fourth Dimension: since he cannot accept the "prophecy" as metaphor, he must disappear into the dimension where it "exists." The demand that his vision be literally true, in other words, requires the Traveller to be no more real than it is; and his return into the Fourth Dimension fulfills this demand.

[17] Pritchett, *The Living Novel* (London, 1946), p. 119.

[18] Probably Henry James's admiration for *The Time Machine* owed much to his recognition of the complexity of its points of view. On January 21, 1900, he wrote to Wells: "It was very graceful of you to send me your book—I mean the particular masterpiece entitled *The Time Machine*, after I had so *un*gracefully sought it at your hands" (*Henry James and H. G. Wells*, ed. Leon Edel and Gordon N. Ray [Urbana, 1958], p. 63).

In being subsumed in his vision, however, he also renders it no less real than any member of his fictive audience; so that the reader, though he is not of course persuaded to take *The Time Machine*'s future as fact, is nevertheless forced to allow the same degree of credibility to the science-fiction "prophecy" as to the "realistic" contemporary scene in which the Traveller relates his story. What the reader is left with, then, is the "prophecy" itself, the metaphorical truth connecting the blind and complacent optimism evidenced by the fictive audience to the resultant devolution envisioned by the Time Traveller.

Far from vitiating the impact of *The Time Machine*, the Traveller's return to the Fourth Dimension thus reinforces the fiction's claim to integrity. By having the Time Traveller act out the ultimate consequence of taking a "prophetic" vision literally, Wells alerts one to the rigor he has submitted himself to in satirizing certain "present ideals." The vision of devolution as the measure of those ideals derives from them—as the Time Traveller's theories indicate—and at the same time contradicts the expectations that they foster, while the response of the fictive audience to the vision corroborates its "prophetic" accuracy.

The Comedy of Limitation

by Patrick Parrinder

There is little doubt that Wells thought of the novel as a more challenging form than the scientific romance. The publication of *Love and Mr. Lewisham* (1900) was greeted, predictably enough, with the suggestion that he had strayed beyond the limits of his talent. "I *will* write novels," he protested to Arnold Bennett; his romances were the freaks of inspiration, but novels were "the proper stuff for my everyday work, a methodical careful distillation of one's thoughts and sentiments and experiences and impressions." [1] Both *Love and Mr. Lewisham* and *Kipps* were the products of constant revision. As Gordon N. Ray has demonstrated in his important study "H. G. Wells Tries to be a Novelist" (1960), Wells at the start of the century was determined to excel at what he had called, in one of a forthright and discriminating series of fiction reviews, "the most vital and typical art of this country and period." Yet the first fruits of his determination were the social comedies—works which have been abundantly loved for their warmth, gaiety, and anarchic humour, but which have rarely engaged the attention of literary critics. Henry James's ambivalent response to *Kipps*—"not so much a masterpiece as a mere born gem" [2]—can be taken as expressing the general opinion. It is true that there is a yawning gap in *Love and Mr. Lewisham*, at least, between the slightness and unevenness of Wells's achievement, and the artistic ambitions which he later recalled: "It was consciously a work of art; it was

[1] *Arnold Bennett & H. G. Wells*, ed. Harris Wilson (London: Hart-Davis, 1960), p. 45.

[2] *Henry James & H. G. Wells*, ed. Leon Edel and Gordon N. Ray (London: Hart-Davis, 1958), p. 105.

designed to be very clear, simple, graceful, and human." [3] But
these terms are fitting enough when we come to the finest of the
comedies, *The History of Mr. Polly* (1910). Here at last Wells wrote
a vital, enduring novel, infused with a sophisticated art beneath
the intuitive surface.

In all his early novels Wells combines the detachment of
comedy with a penetrating study of individual development. In
Love and Mr. Lewisham the mixture is not a happy one. At first the
hero is repeatedly called "Mr. Lewisham," and the narrative is
arch and mannered; by the end he is invariably "he," and he has
become a mouthpiece for Wells's ideas and attitudes. Lewisham
is a poor but gifted science student whose experiences are fairly
close to Wells's own. The result, however unsatisfactory, is at
least a novel in which—as Bernard Shaw wrote of his novel, *The
Irrational Knot*—" the morality is original and not readymade."

The story of Lewisham's life is one of conflict between a career
of possible intellectual attainments and the acceptance of
undistinguished drudgery in support of a wife and family. His
promise as a student fades as he develops a sexual fixation for his
narrow, conventional girl-friend Ethel. He marries her and
subdues himself, later reproaching himself bitterly for the
sacrifice of his ambitions. But this is only adolescent self-pity;
maturity comes through the tutelage of his dubious father-in-law,
the spiritualist medium Chaffery, who writes to him at his lowest
point that "you are having a very good time, you know, fighting
the world." Lewisham at last fully embraces the day-to-day role
of father and breadwinner of a family. The final chapter is
entitled "The Crowning Victory"; he tears up the "Schema" or
programme of his ambitions which had guided the sterile
fact-grubbing of his scholastic years, and turns instead to his
child. It is not that domesticity brings a sense of comfortable
fulfilment. The ideal of self-fulfilment is connected with the
vanity of his career, and in rejecting this Lewisham at last goes
beyond himself, dedicating himself to the general evolutionary
struggle of humanity. The story began with him living in an attic
filled with timetables, certificates, and admonitory slogans.
Stuffy, angular, and unventilated, the attic is a perfect image of

---

[3] *The Atlantic Edition of the Works of H. G. Wells* (London: Unwin, 1924–7), VII,
p. ix.

his mind; its physical shape, with "lead-framed dormer windows, a slanting ceiling and a bulging wall," even bears a shadowy resemblance to his bespectacled face. The view from the windows, and the stirring spring weather outside, are the main threat to his regulated cramming. At the end, however, he is seen in a room described solely in terms of its "spacious outlook" over the bustle of Clapham Junction. His loyalty is now to the dynamic process of life itself. There is an interesting contrast with the ending of Arnold Bennett's first novel, *A Man from the North* (1898), which may be brought out by brief quotations:

> He heard the trot of the child behind him. Children . . . Perhaps a child of his might give sign of literary ability. If so—and surely these instincts descended, were not lost—how he would foster and encourage it! (Bennett).[4] "Come to think, it is all the Child. The future is the Child. The Future. What are we—any of us—but servants or traitors to that? . . ." (Wells). (Ch. 32).

Bennett's failed writer is simply finding consolation in defeat; Lewisham does not postpone the quest but rejects personal ambition altogether. Wells here is dramatising the ethical premise of his biological humanism—a man's individuality is not his complete expression—and the result is somewhat forced and didactic. The status of individuality has earlier been questioned by Chaffery, the demonic *raisonneur* of the novel, under the pretext of a discussion of spiritualism. Full of virtuous indignation, Lewisham has come to denounce his father-in-law's mediumistic frauds. Chaffery welcomes him volubly, and argues that he is a much more consistent socialist than Lewisham, since he cheats the rich rather than deceiving himself. He goes on to attack the naively phenomenal approach of South Kensington science, and to overwhelm his listener with philosophical puzzles:

> "I sometimes think with Bishop Berkeley, that all experience is probably something quite different from reality. That consciousness is *essentially* hallucination. I here, and you, and our talk—it is all Illusion. Bring your Science to bear—what am I? A cloudy multitude of atoms, an infinite interplay of little cells. Is this hand that I hold out, me? This head? Is the surface of my skin any more than a rude average boundary? You say it is my mind that is me? But consider the war of motives. Suppose I have an impulse that I

[4] Arnold Bennett, *A Man from the North* (London: John Lane, 1898), p. 265.

resist—it is *I* resist it—the impulse is outside me, eh? But suppose that impulse carries me and I do the thing—that impulse is part of me, is it not? Ah! My brain reels at these mysteries! Lord! what flimsy fluctuating things we are—first this, then that, a thought, an impulse, a deed and a forgetting, and all the time madly cocksure we are ourselves." (Ch. 23).

Although it forms part of a vivid defence of roguery, Chaffery's scepticism echoes the lessons which Wells had learnt as a biology student and was to expound in his philosophical credo, "Scepticism of the Instrument" (1905).[5] Lewisham soon finds himself the unwilling heir of some of Chaffery's beliefs, as well as of his family responsibilities.

The whole internal development of Wells's hero is a "war of motives." He is "madly cocksure" in the argument about spiritualism, and "madly cocksure" in his intellectual ambitions, and he has to learn to see himself as a "flimsy fluctuating thing" in a larger social and natural process. In spite of his rhetorical appeal to the future, he comes in practice to adopt an excessively defeatist attitude. The bare ideals of survival and persistence belong much more properly in the bleak, post-catastrophe world of *The War in the Air* (1908). Wells later wrote in *Experiment in Autobiography* that the submissiveness of *Love and Mr. Lewisham* betrayed incipient "domestic claustrophobia" in himself. Certainly some timid special pleading was needed to justify Lewisham's parting from Alice Heydinger, the blue-stocking girl who is his last link with the upper world of careerism and success:

> "The thing is, I must simplify my life. I shall do nothing unless I simplify my life. Only people who are well off can be—complex. It is one thing or the other—". (Ch. 31).

Gordon N. Ray points out that the feeling here is echoed in one of Wells's newspaper pieces, a transparent exercise in mock-renunciation called "Excelsior":

> Better a little grocery, a life of sordid anxiety, love, and a tumult of children, than this Dead Sea fruit of success. It is fun to struggle, but tragedy to win.[6]

[5] "Scepticism of the Instrument," a paper read to the Oxford Philosophical Society in 1903, was published as an appendix to *A Modern Utopia* (1905).

[6] Quoted by Gordon N. Ray, "H. G. Wells Tries to be a Novelist" in *Edwardians and Late Victorians*, ed. Richard Ellmann (New York: Columbia University Press, 1960), pp. 121, 127.

Lewisham is deliberately sent down into this limited, lower-class world. Wells was both deeply aware of the divisiveness of Victorian class consciousness, and divided himself in his attitude to the world he had left. The conflict could not be resolved through an articulate, naturally complex figure like Lewisham; Wells may have been in a similar position to Lewisham in the obscure years of his first marriage (1891–3), but he did not submit to "simplicity" for long. In his other social novels lower-class life takes a more sinister aspect. In *The Wonderful Visit* the villagers are said to be "pithed" in their formative years, so that they accept their allotted stations; and the spectre of the manipulative and compressive education of the Selenites in *The First Men in the Moon* stands behind the portrayal of individual development in *Kipps* and *Mr. Polly*. Polly is compared to a rabbit in a trap, and one of Kipps's fellow-apprentices declares bitterly: "we're in a blessed drain-pipe, and we've got to crawl along it till we die." In these books the experience of the simple hero, the "little man" confined in the nets of the retail trade, is revealed and interpreted by a complex narrator addressing the reader from what Wells elsewhere called "our educated standpoint."[7] This interplay of narrator and character leads to an opposition of worlds similar to that in the scientific romances. The alternating images of deterministic and utopian life that we find in the romances are now seen against the class structure of English society. The comedy arises from a confrontation between the class into which Wells was born and the class into which he adventured, and it leads towards a new world of escape from the limitations of either.

The first and least substantial of his comic heroes is Hoopdriver, the draper's assistant in *The Wheels of Chance* (1896). This "Holiday Adventure" is constructed around a cycling tour of southern England. Hoopdriver, enjoying his annual ten days of freedom, is released into an idyllic world where class distinctions temporarily disappear, and he becomes involved in a fragile and sentimental intrigue with a middle-class girl. *The Wheels of Chance* has a period charm, as a record of the home counties undisturbed by the motor-car, but its high spirits are deadened by the facetiousness of the prose style which Wells had developed for his

[7] "Two Views of Life" in *Saturday Review*, LXXIX (1895), p. 676.

humorous sketches in the *Pall Mall Gazette*. (*Certain Personal Matters* is a representative selection of these.) The humour is choked by the assumptions of respectability; writer and reader are assumed to be familiar only with the customer's side of the counter, and Wells is torn between the impulse to express Hoopdriver's experience and the impulse to disown all kinship with him. During 1903–4, he returned to *The Wheels of Chance* and produced a dramatised version, entitled *Hoopdriver's Holiday*. This was never performed, and was only published in 1964, with an introduction by Michael Timko indicating that Wells for a time had serious thoughts of becoming a dramatist. In *Hoopdriver's Holiday*, he turned a cautious, lightweight comedy into something approaching a social problem play. Just before the final curtain Hoopdriver is left alone on the stage, bitterly denouncing the middle-class family who have just cold-shouldered him, and the social system in general:

> "It isn't fair! It isn't fair! I never 'ad a chance! I was shoved into that shop before I was fourteen. I got no education. . . . I got no ideas! Fourteen. . . . When 'er sort of chaps are going off to their Etons and their 'Arrows. And then they turn and scoff at you! What am I? I'm a thing to measure linen and pack parcels. . . . a sort of white nigger! Me in Sydenham!. . . . A country ought to be ashamed to turn out a man like me. I'm done for. I've woke up too late! What can I do now?" (*Moment of perfect meditation.*) "I'll do *something*. . . . If I kill myself to do it!" (*He turns about as if seeking for something to do.*)
>
> *Curtain*[8]

This is raw and crude as drama, but it shows Wells drawing in a much wider range of feelings than in *The Wheels of Chance*. Anger and social protest are the essential preliminaries to his mature comedy.

In *Kipps* (1905) they are transmuted into the brilliant portrayal of the hero's childhood and apprenticeship. At the beginning Kipps is free, open and undefined. His parents have died in unspecified circumstances, leaving only a few vague memories, and he lives with an uncle and aunt who are remote, inanimate figures. But he is the nucleus of a marvellously solid and tangible little world:

[8] *Hoopdriver's Holiday*, ed. Michael Timko (*English Literature in Transition*: Purdue University, Indiana, 1964), p. 77.

He knew all the stones in the yard individually, the creeper in the
corner, the dustbin and the mossy wall, better than many men
know the faces of their wives. There was a corner under the
ironing-board which, by means of a shawl, could be made, under
propitious gods, a very decent cubby-house, a corner that served
him for several years as the indisputable hub of the world, and the
stringy places in the carpet, the knots upon the dresser, and the
several corners of the rag hearthrug his uncle had made, became
essential parts of his mental foundations. (Bk. I, Ch. 1).

These are the earliest data of his being. Both here and in his story
"The Door in the Wall," Wells's view of childhood may be
compared to Wordsworth's. The child is not altogether dissociated from his environment; later, the prison-house shades
descend. At first Kipps's fluid individuality expresses itself in a
rich variety of roles—he plays at red Indians, warriors, ship-
wrecked sailors, and smugglers. But soon a straitjacket of social
conventions and prohibitions is imposed upon him, until the
broad sympathies of his early imaginative life become atrophied
and perverted. The process begins with some painful lessons in
table manners and continues at school, but full-scale subjugation
only begins when he enters the drapery at Folkestone. *Kipps*
contains Wells's fullest and bitterest description of the apprentice's life. The conditions are those which he himself knew, but
they undergo a creative transformation comparable to that
which Dickens wrought on the social institutions in his novels.
Kipps's first tour of the Emporium with the proprietor has a
hallucinatory quality. Shalford prides himself on his "System,"
an attempt to regulate his business as if it were a clockwork
mechanism, by means of petty rules, a strict hierarchy, and
penny-pinching economies. As each employee becomes aware of
the boss's approach, he snaps into his position in the "System,"
"exactly like an automaton that is suddenly set going," and
Kipps's split-second vision of them in the privacy of their own
activities takes on the unreality of an optical illusion. The theme
of dehumanisation is pursued in Carshot, forever murmuring
"My Heart and Liver"; in Shalford's notices which always end
"By Order"; and in his mutilation of language into a system of
commercial telegraphese. Kipps, who at first has "no more
System than a bad potato," is eventually worn down into
submission. It is a cramped and limited life. There are certain

measures of enjoyment and self-development—flirtations with
the Emporium's young ladies, learning refinement and becoming
a "Masher," and even attending woodwork classes. Individuality
of a kind lives on in the spirited uncouthness which is the only
remnant of his childhood imaginative state. But these things are
circumscribed by our knowledge of his situation. Kipps has been
broken into his place in society, and he is a fully-formed draper.

This is only part of the story, however, and indeed *Kipps* was
originally conceived as a great comic panorama entitled *The
Wealth of Mr. Waddy.*[9] Only a third of the original material
survived in the published form. It is the only one of Wells's novels
to employ a conventional Victorian plot structure. Since the
drapery is represented as a lifelong dead end, Kipps clearly has
to escape somehow, and this is contrived through the discovery
that he is the heir of a Mr. Waddy. Suddenly he finds himself a
man of means and leisure, the owner of a house on the sea front,
and an eligible bachelor. He becomes an unnaturally good
bourgeois, punctilious in his observation of the preposterous
genteel conventions and eagerly exchanging his freedom for the
new bondage of afternoon calls, dinner parties and smart hotels.
Wells, in fact, takes his hero on a comic journey through the
English class system. A rebellion against the social traps that are
laid for him becomes inevitable. It is prepared for by the revival
of his childhood romance with the girl next door, Ann Pornick,
and by his meeting with her brother and his friend Masterman—
exponents of socialism whose function is to suggest the violence
and greed beneath the mannered surface of genteel society.
When Kipps does rebel, he plunges through the surface and
returns to the homely simplicity of Ann. After further adven-
tures, the tale of frustrations and humiliations is over, and he
ends up happily as a country bookseller. *Kipps* is a sprawling,
capacious novel in the Dickens mode, a mixture of comedy of
manners, *Bildungsroman*, socialist tract, and modern folk-tale (the
last element being virtually all that survived in the musical
adaptation, *Half a Sixpence*). It is held together by Wells's most
characteristic structural device, the cycle of suppression and

---

[9] An early draft of *Kipps*, based on Wells's 1899 typescript, has recently been
published: *The Wealth of Mr. Waddy*, ed. Harris Wilson (Carbondale &
Edwardsville: Southern Illinois University Press, 1969).

release. Twice Kipps frees himself from claustrophobic social confinement, in acts of energetic and anarchic rebellion. He owes the first escape to his legacy, but this stroke of luck is a direct consequence of the wild, drunken night which leads to dismissal from the drapery. The second escape occurs when Kipps breaks out of a dinner party, and rushes down to the servants' quarters to propose to Ann, threatening to throw himself off the pier if she rejects him. These melodramatic acts are paralleled in Wells's story, "The Purple Pileus," where the henpecked shopkeeper, Mr. Coombes, attempts to commit suicide by eating toadstools. But instead of poisoning him, they transform him into a raving fury of self-assertion. This is not a story of any great moral depth; Coombes's escapade simply makes him a more masterful husband. But the pattern is repeated with much greater intensity in *Mr. Polly*, where the great Fishbourne fire burns out the traces of the hero's mental subjection. "The Door in the Wall" is another of these stories of individual release. In each case Wells depicts an unforeseen rebellion against society and its appointed roles, a rebellion of the Freudian id against the ego and superego, with the character freeing himself through an act of self-destructive abandon. The pattern of individual release culminates in *Mr. Polly*, where it leads to a deliverance from the deterministic world with revolutionary implications. "If the world does not please you, *you can change it*," he discovers.

In making Kipps and Polly symbolic figures whose individual actions follow a representative pattern, Wells was departing considerably from the norm of realistic portrayal. His characters are evidently stylised; A. J. P. Taylor has described them disapprovingly as "caricatures or Humours" rather than real people,[10] implying that Wells was a victim of the distortions inherent in the comic sense of life. In an interesting essay by John Holms (1928), Wells's sole literary achievement was found to be the begetting of an "authentic comic creation," the figure of the "little man."[11] Neither critic suggests the terms in which we could discriminate between different orders of caricature or

[10] A. J. P. Taylor, "The Man who tried to work Miracles," in *The Listener*, 21 July 1966, p. 81.

[11] John Holms, "H. G. Wells" in *Scrutinies*, ed. Edgell Rickword (London: Wishart, 1928), p. 149.

comic creation; between Polly and the figures in a *Punch* cartoon,
or his contemporary Billy Bunter. The condition which all these
figures have in common is the detached and external viewpoint
from which they are seen, so that they tend to become
object-lessons. But detachment can lead to anything from a jeer
to a poem or a system of sociology. In Wells at his best, there is a
play of observation around his character which is both intellectually considered and imaginatively profound.

His method of characterisation expresses his scientific as well
as his comic instincts. Henry James wrote to him that in *Kipps* he
had "handled [the English lower-middle class] vulgarity in so
scientific and historic a spirit," avoiding the picturesque and
romantic "interference" of Dickens, Thackeray, and George
Eliot. This is a remarkable claim, which few would take at its
face value. The late nineteenth century saw a widespread
reaction against narrative "interference." Novelists after Flaubert sought to achieve an enhancement of realism through the
discipline of artistic impersonality—the novelist as camera-eye
rather than the novelist as puppet-master. No English-speaking
novelist was more deeply interested in this movement than James
himself. Wells, on the other hand, roundly attacked what he
called the " 'colourless' theory of fiction," declaring that "The
theory of a scientific, an impersonal standpoint, is fallacious." [12]
He preferred the discursive, moralising commentary used by the
Victorians, and this led him into frequent wrangles with Arnold
Bennett, who accused him of artistic conservatism. His claim to
be considered a "scientific" novelist, in fact, lies in the nature of
his personal intrusions and not in their absence. James must have
meant that he had given a closer and more objective explanation
of his own class than had been achieved before; it is as if he were
an anthropologist, or one of his own scientific explorers, bringing
back news of the strange tribe whom James saw on his daily
walks. The comedies abound in moments of pointed observation,
picked out with Wells's unfailing eye for the typical; no modern
novelist has caught the savour of English social consciousness
more acutely. There is Old Kipps, who falls in rapidly with the

[12] See his reviews of Gissing's *The Paying Guest* and Meredith's *The Amazing
Marriage*, respectively: *Saturday Review*, LXXXI (1896), p. 405 and LXXX
(1895), p. 843.

revised ambitions caused by his nephew's private income: "Y'ought to 'ave a bit o' shootin' somewheer." And a snatch of dialogue which shows how society helps its exploited shop-assistants to achieve self-respect:

> Buggins resumed reading. He was very much excited by a leader on Indian affairs. "By Jove!" he said, "it won't do to give these here Blacks votes."
>
> "No fear," said Kipps.
>
> "They're different altogether," said Buggins. "They 'aven't the sound sense of Englishmen, and they 'aven't the character. There's a sort of tricky dishonesty about 'em—false witness and all that—of which an Englishman has no idea. Outside their courts of law—it's a pos'tive fact, Kipps—there's witnesses waitin' to be 'ired. Reg'lar trade. Touch their 'ats as you go in. Englishmen 'ave no idea, I tell you—not ord'nary Englishmen. It's in their blood. They're too timid to be honest. Too slavish. They aren't used to being free like we are, and if you gave 'em freedom they wouldn't make a proper use of it. Now, *we*—Oh, *Damn!*"
>
> For the gas had suddenly gone out, and Buggins had the whole column of Society Club Chat still to read. (Bk. I Ch. 6).

It is lights out in the Emporium: but as long as you can read the *Daily World Manager* for an hour or so beforehand, you know that you are free. This is a comedy based, not on individual eccentricities, but on the supposition that men are unconsciously circumscribed and controlled by their social environment. Wells takes a taxonomic view of character, arranging and classifying it according to larger generalisations. His "scientific" aims, which place him with Flaubert and James, are summed up in a phrase from *Tono-Bungay*—"social comparative anatomy." The opening sentences of *Tono-Bungay* contain Wells's principal statement of the taxonomic attitude. The speaker is George Ponderevo, the hero-narrator:

> Most people in this world seem to live "in character"; they have a beginning, a middle and an end, and the three are congruous one with another and true to the rules of their type. You can speak of them as being of this sort of people or that. They are, as theatrical people say, no more (and no less) than "character actors." They have a class, they have a place, they know what is becoming in them and what is due to them, and their proper size of tombstone tells at last how properly they have played the part. But there is also another kind of life that is not so much living as a

> miscellaneous tasting of life. One gets hit by some unusual
> transverse force, one is jerked out of one's stratum and lives
> crosswise for the rest of the time, and, as it were, in a succession of
> samples. That has been my lot, and that is what has set me at last
> writing something in the nature of a novel.

Society turns its members into "character actors" playing
predetermined roles; the novelist is aware of this process, which
he himself has managed to evade. Wells's indifference to the
conventional wisdom of the novel in his day is strongly evident
here. The inherent dangers of an excessively schematic attitude
to character were realised in most of his later novels. But in the
early comedies and in *Tono-Bungay* he made the "sociological
novel" into a wholly imaginative form. Minor characters like
Buggins and Old Kipps are both living "in character," and the
size of their tombstones may already be predicted. Of young
Kipps, too, Wells writes that after a time at the Emporium his
sorrows "grew less acute, and, save for a miracle, the brief
tragedy of his life was over." It takes a complex, scientific
intelligence to comprehend the limitations of ordinary people.
George Ponderevo's "miscellaneous tasting of life" has produced
this superior awareness, at least in a provisional form. Wells had
had the same opportunities, and it is no accident that George is
shown as a natural novelist. Kipps and Polly are also hit by a
"transverse force" and jerked crosswise. They become conscious
of their subservience, but after the brief moment of rebellion and
displacement they settle down in a new "character" which is
equally fixed and yet capacious enough for them to fill in
comfort. This individual transfiguration solves no social problems. It is simply the discovery of an oasis of undisturbed
happiness within the desert of oppression. Kipps ends up in a
small shop, having lost most of his fortune; he would be in
financial trouble but for a lucky investment with a struggling
playwright. The shop is a sort of pastoral no-man's land between
the frontiers of leisured gentility and those of economic subjection.
The suggestion of pastoral is expanded in *Mr. Polly*, where the grey
realities of the hero's early life give way to the Potwell Inn and
a lyrical vision of an England steeped in utopian primitivism.

Kipps ends with a receding and patronising effect which is too
distinctly Edwardian in tone to be very acceptable today. Almost
the last words are Kipps's recognition of his own uniqueness: "I

don't suppose there ever was a chap quite like me before."
Richard Ellmann, who sees the hero's journey as a quest for
self-fulfilment, has written that "He is himself at last." [13] This
would be out of tune with the didactic ending of *Love and Mr.
Lewisham*, and, in fact, we do not see Kipps achieving self-discovery. As David Lodge says in a highly suggestive article, there is a
"hollow note" [14] to the comedy. Wells intrudes with a narrative
aside ("I am an old and trusted customer now"), affirming the
truth of Kipps's story. The hero is now a carefully distanced
small shopkeeper who still splutters out his words in heavily
accentuated cockney. We see him, in the words of the book's
subtitle, as a "Simple Soul." He has found a way of life and the
sense of tranquillity, but there is and will always be a complex
dimension of living which eludes his awareness:

> Out of the darkness beneath the shallow weedy stream of his
> being rose a question, a question that looked up dimly and never
> reached the surface. It was the question of the wonder of the
> beauty, the purposeless, inconsecutive beauty, that falls so
> strangely among the happenings and memories of life. It never
> reached the surface of his mind, it never took to itself substance or
> form; it looked up merely as the phantom of a face might look, out
> of deep waters, and sank again into nothingness. (Bk. III Ch. 3).

The rather too misty and picturesque image seems to be put in
for Kipps's benefit, and writer and reader are felt to be better
equipped to articulate the question than he is. But the passage
also has the sense that before the fundamental question of life we
are all on the same level. An impression of parity between
narrator and hero is essential for the success of this comic
method, and it is much more securely achieved in *Mr. Polly*. In
the following passage the narrator is still a controlling presence,
but the flow of sympathy is as strong as the sense of detachment:

> He came to country inns and sat for unmeasured hours talking of
> this and that to those sage carters who rest for ever in the taps of
> the country inns, while the big, sleek, brass-jingling horses wait
> patiently outside with their wagons. He got a job with some van
> people who were wandering about the country with swings and a

[13] Richard Ellmann, "Two Faces of Edward" in *Edwardians and Late Victorians*,
ed. Ellmann (New York: Columbia University Press, 1960), p. 199.
[14] David Lodge, "Assessing H. G. Wells" in *The Novelist at the Crossroads*
(London: Routledge & Kegan Paul, 1971), p. 217.

steam roundabout, and remained with them three days, until one
of their dogs took a violent dislike to him, and made his duties
unpleasant. He talked to tramps and wayside labourers. He
snoozed under hedges by day, and in outhouses and hayricks at
night, and once, but only once, he slept in a casual ward. He felt
as the etiolated grass and daisies must do when you move the
garden roller away to a new place. (Ch. 9).

Most of this is plain, apparently neutral narrative, with the slow
prose-rhythms suggesting the somnolent and regular passage of
time in this half-idyllic rural world. The right moment for the
personal intrusion is carefully chosen; it harmonises perfectly
with the preceding description, and yet firmly and authorita-
tively interprets Polly in his released state, adding to his
imaginative dimensions: "He felt as the etiolated grass and
daisies must do when you move the garden roller away to a new
place." This is a fresh variation on the theme of naturalness, and
also a microcosm of the interpretation of life and the scale of
values which inform *Mr. Polly* as a whole. The garden roller is
society, and once it is off his back he can continue to grow
untrammelled. At such a moment the character makes a jump
into immediacy, focusing our attention on the act of imaginative
invention itself. At its best, this narrative method does not set the
characters free, but enacts a series of renewals of their original
setting-forth in the author's mind. The result is an interplay
between third person narrator and simple hero, which in turn
produces an interplay of social and personal assumptions. Wells
both sees his hero from above, and sees with him from below; he
measures his limitations from outside, and presents his vitality
from inside. In this transmutation of his attitude to his own
earlier life as a draper's apprentice, there is a curious mixture of
collectivism and individualism. The taxonomic narrative empha-
sises the hero's relative simplicity and typicality; but at the same
time Wells makes solitary heroes out of people whom most
novelists would relegate to a subordinate role. Dickens created
many communities of minor lower-class characters, but there is
no Dickens hero who does not establish his connexions with the
gentry. Nor are Kipps and Polly redeemed by the intellectual
gifts, the articulateness or the fine moral insight of so many
modern protagonists. In playing the spotlight of the novel on the
comedy and poignancy of essentially limited lives, Wells was
doing something genuinely new.

Wells as Edwardian

by William Bellamy

I

H. G. Wells is the greatest of the modern global therapists; nobody else, indeed, has seemed to want the publicity of being, in an age of public exposure, a prophet so vulnerable. But the millennial unity that Wells imagined and fought for is something taken almost for granted in the computerese of Marshall McLuhan. While Wells was perhaps the last important "thinker" to attempt to confront a "sequential" universe, and was caught up to the last printed utterance of his life in the disordered conflict between fears and wishes in the face of the future, Philip Rieff, for example, announces "a fundamental change of focus in the entire cast of our culture—toward a human condition about which there will be nothing further to say in terms of the old style of despair and hope." [1] We may return to Rieff again and again as we examine the therapeutic crisis of Wells, not as to some new prophetical absolute (in whom we put all trust and faith) but as a focus point for ironical contrast with Wells.

Perhaps Wells is more important as the writer who could be passionately either an optimist or a pessimist than as one or the other exclusively. For in his application of alternative fantasies of Utopia and anti-Utopia he is the very archetype of bemused pre-Rieffian, pre-McLuhan, man. It may be, indeed, that Wells's "optimism" and "pessimism" are not separate states indicative of

---

"Wells as Edwardian" (editor's title). From William Bellamy, *The Novels of Wells, Bennett and Galsworthy* (London: Routledge & Kegan Paul Ltd, 1971). Copyright © 1971 by William Bellamy. Reprinted by permission of the author and the publisher.

[1] *The Triumph of the Therapeutic*, London, 1966, 261.

some radical inconsistency, but are complementary attitudes. As Frank Kermode has suggested:

> In general, we seem to combine a sense of decadence in society—as evidenced by the concept of alienation, which, supported by a new interest in the early Marx, has never enjoyed more esteem—with a technological utopianism. In our ways of thinking about the future there are contradictions which if we were willing to consider them openly, might call for some effort towards complementarity. But they lie, as a rule, too deep.[2]

Equipped as we are to trace the connection between the post-cultural state and the mixture of freeing and alienation that it involves, we may perhaps understand more clearly the Utopianizing role played by Wellsian characters like Bert Smallways:

> Bert Smallways was a vulgar little creature, the sort of pert, limited soul that the old civilization of the early twentieth century produced by the million in every country of the world. He had lived all his life in narrow streets, and between mean houses he could not look over, and in a narrow circle of ideas from which there was no escape. . . . Now by a curious accident he found himself lifted out of his marvellous modern world for a time, out of all the rush and confused appeals of it, and floating like a thing dead and disembodied between sea and sky. It was as if Heaven was experimenting with him, had picked him out as a sample from the English millions to look at him more nearly and to see what was happening to the soul of man.[3]

Bert Smallways's transcendental experience in a world without God is the archetypal experience of Wells's post-1900 heroes. Although Wells's Edwardian novels have in common a direct, outward-looking interest in "society," they nevertheless focus that interest by rendering the disengaged consciousnesses of ordinary men. Often this discrepancy between the isolated consciousness and the "old-fashioned" cultural limitations of its societal environment is the source of some excellent comedy, which is exploited as a method for showing the pressures operating upon dissociated existence, upon existential man.

However much a Wells book may seem to be concerned with

[2] *The Sense of an Ending*, New York, 1967, 100.
[3] *The War in the Air*, London, 1908, 67–8.

society on a large scale, as in *Tono-Bungay* or *The War of the Worlds,* it derives its force and originality from the rhythm of personal Utopianization that runs through it. Whether Wells is concerned primarily with social ideas or with the plight of an individual, he generally presents, in his pre-1910 novels, a therapeutic process containing one main character. In the early novels the process tends to be conformative, and the therapy implemented by Griffin, for example, is negative. In the post-1900 novels, and certainly in the novels from *Kipps* (1905) and *In the Days of the Comet* (1906) onwards, the therapeutic pattern tends to be positively Utopianizing and transformative.

In Bert Smallways the pattern of desocialized, "disembodied," post-cultural existence recurs. In his deculturalized state he is "like a thing dead," but he has a cosmic involvement unknown to the millions of "limited" souls: "It was as if Heaven was experimenting with him." The analytic attitude which the narrative of the novel forthwith displays is the attitude necessary for survival in the limbo beyond culture. Only a transformative activism can effect the cosmic Utopianization which is seen to have occurred in, for example, the last pages of *Mr. Polly*:

> Polly sat beside the fat woman at one of the little green tables at the back of the Potwell Inn. . . . It was as if everything lay securely within a great, warm, friendly globe of crystal sky. It was as safe and enclosed and fearless as a child that has still to be born.[4]

II

In the Days of the Comet is divided into two parts: in the first the lower-class Leadford is driven to desperation when his beloved Nettie has a love affair with the upper-class Verrall. He sets out to murder them both. At the very climax of the murder-hunt, the apocalyptic comet effects a global "Change" in human psychology, and a new sense of "well-being" and rationality descends upon all the characters of the novel. A Wellsian *ménage à trois,* rationally managed, is the outcome. The new triumph of the rational ego is associated with a widespread communalization of society.

[4] *The History of Mr. Polly*, London, 1910, 368.

In the Days of the Comet is thus radically different from the science-fiction novels of the 1890s. It might be seen as a way of talking about the transition from pressurized *fin-de-siècle* time to the post-1900 experience of "redeemed" time. Its time-structure is interestingly similar, in fact, to *The Winter's Tale* (which may also, of course, relate to the experience of living through the turning of an important century).

In this novel of 1906 a para-Freudian analytic therapy is set up as the cure for cultural crisis. Frank Wells has drawn attention to the existence of the characters in the book "beyond culture":

> This novel is . . . a touchpaper to set off a rocket of discussion, ideas and argument. The characters are not inhabitants of the Five Towns, as are the living characters of Arnold Bennett, they are "world" characters—strangely English.[5]

This usefully emphasizes H. G. Wells's sense of the incongruousness of the residual cultural characteristics of his post-cultural characters; but only in the second half of the book is Frank Wells's second sentence strictly applicable. In the first half of the book the murderous intensity with which Leadford pursues his class-hatred is depicted strictly—though, indeed, crudely—in a specifically English milieu, with the social divisions which Wells saw characterizing that milieu depicted in some "cultural" detail. Seen in this light, Leadford is initially an *alter ego* of Kipps's. Only after the comet has effected its change does the "citizen of the World" character of Leadford emerge.[6]

Wells's depiction of Leadford in a pre-apocalyptic state of cultural repression, driven into an irrational murderous rage by the exigencies of contemporary society, may bear resemblances to the state of Wells's mind before 1900 and indeed to the psychic condition of the late-Victorian period as a whole. Leadford, writing of an imminent fictional war with Germany from his post-apocalyptic vantage-point, defines himself in much the same

[5] Collins edition, London, 1954, 15.

[6] I should want, also, to suggest that Edwin Clayhanger is presented by Arnold Bennett as, in a sense, quite as much a "world" character as Wells's Leadford. Edwin's "culturation," his "Five-Townsiness," is as incongruous in him, finally, as Leadford's Englishness is in Leadford. It is not in culture but by revolutionizing a private universe beyond culture that Edwin finds salvation in life. And to suggest that the "living" characters of Arnold Bennett are *more* living than Leadford is to make a critical decision that requires some testing.

way as the symptomatics of the 1890s unconsciously defined
themselves:

> It was like one of a flood of disease germs that have invaded a
> body, that paper.[7] There I was, one corpuscle in the big
> amorphous body of the English community, one of forty-one
> million such corpuscles; and, for all my preoccupations, these
> potent headlines, this paper ferment, caught me and swung me
> about. And all over the country that day, millions read as I read,
> and came into line with me, under the same magnetic spell, came
> round—how did we say it?—Ah!—"to face the foe." [8]

Here Wells is defining *fin-de-siècle* crisis in terms of a disease of
society, and relating the sense of apocalypse to a synthesis of
war-feeling. As in much of the pre-1900 writing of Wells, Bennett
and Galsworthy, Leadford's translation here of the *fin-de-siècle*
experience gives the impression that men felt themselves to be
under the influence of magic, as if afflicted by a voodoo charm.
The words, "magnetic spell," are suggestive of the very heavily
"determined" state of Western thinking in the years just before
calendar apocalypse. In this novel of 1906 (which perhaps
reflects the apocalyptic "disconfirmation" provided to a degree
by the outcome of the Boer War), news of the coming war results
in the comet's being "driven into obscurity overleaf" (p. 94), just
as information about the coming freeing to be derived from
passing through the year 1900 was hidden by the "disease germs"
of *fin de sièclism*.

Again, the state of Leadford after the comet has passed seems
exactly to match Wells's consciousness after 1900; the transition
is made in Wells's fiction from a preoccupation with isolated
individuals in desperate states to a speculative concern for the
quality of individual life within society as a whole. As soon as
Leadford wakes up from the short sleep induced by the comet, he
meets Melmount, one of the fifteen men who are supposed to
have been controlling the Empire and thus have been responsible for the German war. Leadford is thus, by coincidence, introduced to the first sane (i.e. Wellsian) meeting between the
statesmen:

> And what a strange unprecedented thing was that cabinet council
> at which I was present, the council that was held two days later in

---

[7] The *"New Paper."*

[8] Collins edition, 94. Further references to this book are put in parenthesis in
the text.

Melmount's bungalow, and which convened the conference to
frame the constitution of the World State (p. 188).

Nothing could be more naïvely the projection of a writer's own
personal wishes than this, and the lack of artistic tact with which
Wells frames this section is analogous to (though not simultane-
ous with) the general movement in Wells's own development
from artist to therapist impatient of art. It would be easy to
accuse the second section of the novel of being mere discursive
polemic, even less patiently "realized" than the first half. But if
there is naïveté in Wells's account of the changes wrought by the
comet (and indeed of the initial "spell" upon Leadford), the
naïve (in the Kermodean sense) apocalypse of the 1890s and
the sense of a beginning in the 1900s *were* absurdly, childishly,
structured out of the gullibility of men projecting, as Kermode
would say, their existential anxieties upon a centurial ending.
Thus, although Wells's novel is objective enough to depict the
turning into a new era with some justice, it partakes of some of
the simple-mindedness of the immediately post-1900 period. It
positively takes simple-mindedness to be a sign of health.

It is possible to relate Leadford's sense of dispossession and his
alienation before the advent of the comet to the tradition of
alienation that has gradually come to assume a para-cultural
role, being one of the ways in which "literate" people now make
sense of life. The concomitant of alienation is therapy, and it is
also tempting to relate Leadford's sense of "well-being" (p. 153)
after the "Change" to our own nostalgia for health, to the
health-ideal implicit in our own constant diagnosing of contemporary sickness. Before the change, Leadford's determination to
murder Verrall is nihilistic (involving self-destruction), similar to
Mr. Polly's decision to set fire to his shop:

> From that moment when I insulted old Mrs. Verrall I became
> representative. I was a man who stood for all the disinherited of
> the world. I had no hope of pride or pleasure left in me. I was
> raging rebellion against God and mankind. There were no more
> vague intentions swaying me this way and that; I was perfectly
> clear now upon what I meant to do. I would make my protest and
> die (p. 111).

Leadford's predicament seems also to parallel Griffin's in *The
Invisible Man*, and it is significant that once again conscious man's

position is seen to be that of "the disinherited." We have seen
how this state of mind is defined in terms of "germs" and
"sickness." The post-apocalyptic state of Leadford is as clearly
defined as "well-being," and the return to health involves a
return to "the barley-fields of God." The intimate association of
Revelation with regained health is unmistakable:

> I seemed to awaken out of a refreshing sleep. I did not awaken
> with a start, but opened my eyes, and lay very comfortably
> looking at a line of extraordinary scarlet poppies that glowed
> against a glowing sky. It was the sky of a magnificent sunrise, and
> an archipelago of gold-beached purple islands floated in a sea of
> golden-green. The poppies, too, swan-necked buds, blazing corol-
> las, translucent stout seed-vessels, stoutly upheld, had a luminous
> quality, seemed wrought only from some more solid kind of
> light. . . .
> I felt very light, full of the sense of physical well-being. I
> perceived I was lying on my side in a little trampled space in a
> weedy, flowering barley-field, that was in some inexplicable way
> saturated with light and beauty. I sat up and remained for a long
> time filled with the delight and charm of the delicate little
> convolvulus that twined among the barley stems, the pimpernel
> that laced the ground below. . . .
> I felt as though I was a thing in some very luminous painted
> window, as though this dawn broke through me. I felt I was part
> of some exquisite painting painted in light and joy. . . .
> . . . I felt sure I was dead; no one living could have this perfect
> assurance of good, this strong and confident peace. I had made an
> end of the fever called living. . . .
> These, then, must be the barley-fields of God! (pp. 153–5).

This is, aesthetically, a most complex passage, but it should be
possible to establish that the "Luminism" which helps to define
the scene significantly as a dawning is not the style of French
Impressionism, but belongs to another tradition. The passage
surely reflects the Edwardian assimilation of the Renaissance,
and a new transfiguration of man:

> I held up my left hand and arm before me, a grubby hand, a
> frayed cuff; but with a quality of painted unreality, transfigured
> as a beggar might have been by Botticelli. I looked for a time
> steadfastly at a beautiful pearl sleeve link (p. 154).

Such a vision exemplifies the characteristic Edwardian Utopianization of self; written in a prose-style which is a strange mixture of stock image and pseudo-scientific originality, it reflects a disdain for traditional cultural usage which is entirely in keeping with its rendering of the state which exists beyond culture. The phenomenon involved is a post-1900 infilling of the Victorian hollow universe; and, like the Renaissance, this man-made apocalypse is vitally concerned with revivification. There is a connection between this vision of "a magnificent sunrise" and the passage from *The First Men in the Moon* which is cited by Bernard Bergonzi in *The Early H. G. Wells*:

> One after another all down the sunlit slope these miraculous little brown bodies burst and gaped apart, like seed-pods, like the husks of fruits; opened eager mouths that drank in the heat and light pouring in a cascade from the newly-risen sun.
>
> Every moment more of these seed coats ruptured, and even as they did so the swelling pioneers overflowed their rent, distended seed-cases and passed into the second stage of growth. With a steady assurance, a swift deliberation, these amazing seeds thrust a rootlet downward to the earth and a queer bundle-like bud into the air. In a little while the slope was dotted with minute plantlets standing at attention in the blaze of the sun.
>
> They did not stand for long. The bundle-like buds swelled and strained and opened with a jerk, thrusting out a coronet of little sharp tips, spreading a whorl of tiny, spiky, brownish leaves, that lengthened rapidly, lengthened visibly even as we watched. The movement was slower than any animal's, swifter than any plant's I have ever seen before.[9]

Bergonzi attempts to account for the difference between this kind of writing and the earlier "imaginative" prose of the pre-1900 scientific romances. He concludes: "In describing the imaginary panic in London following the Martian invasion, Wells was making certain implications about the society he lived in; in describing the equally imaginary blossoming of the lunar flowers, he was simply exercising his imagination for its own sake." [10] If we search for Bergonzi's idea of the "implications" of *The War of the Worlds*, we find this: "*The War of the Worlds* enacts the secret fears and lack of confidence of late Victorian bourgeois society." [11] In the light of this explanation, it seems unlikely that

[9] *The First Men in the Moon*, London, 1901, 88–9.
[10] *The Early H. G. Wells*, Manchester, 1961, 160.
[11] *Ibid.,* 144.

Wells's description of the moon-flowers was an exercising of the imagination "for its own sake," however; it surely represents, on the contrary, an attitude to the future strikingly opposite to that implicit in *The War of the Worlds*. It depicts the reverse of "lack of confidence" in its rendering of "steady assurance"; and "secret fears" are replaced by "a swift deliberation." In place of the conformative landscapes of *The Time Machine*, we find the transformative landscape of the moon and the barley-fields of God. Bergonzi draws attention to a difference between the early and later work, but his description is more useful if the post-1900 sense of a Utopianizing beginning is recognized:

> In the lunar scenes Wells was able to describe a strange and exotic world with the confidence in his own powers that he had displayed in *The Time Machine*. Indeed, many of these scenes show more exuberance of imagination—particularly visual imagination—than any other passages of Wells's writings. In *The Time Machine* the world of 802701 is vividly realized, but for all the strangeness of detail, the contemporary Southern English landscape is somehow apparent through the great cultivated garden in which the Eloi live. The lunar landscapes are, in one sense, wholly "artificial." [12]

Bergonzi does not deal with *In the Days of the Comet*, which he believes to be a "very inferior novel," [13] but he might perhaps agree that there is some evidence of "exuberance of imagination —particularly visual imagination" in the "barley-fields of God" passage. And the special quality of the "scientific" prose there might indeed be explained by saying that it constructed "artificial" landscapes. After the *fin-de-siècle* depiction of post-cultural man in crisis, hollow and inhabiting a hollow universe, comes the Edwardian creation of a "psychomorphous" universe. A willed intervention in "creative evolution" replaces the self-depriving mode of conformative adaptation. In the section immediately preceding that quoted by Bergonzi, Bedford and Cavor undergo an experience which seems to parallel this transition from the dead, mechanical universe of Darwinian process to the Bergsonian Vitalism of the post-1900 world:

> How can I describe the thing I saw? It is so petty a thing to state, and yet it seemed so wonderful, so pregnant with emotion. I have

[12] *Ibid.*, 159.
[13] *Ibid.*, 75.

said that amidst the stick-like litter were these rounded bodies, these little oval bodies that might have passed as very small pebbles. And now first one and then another had stirred, had rolled over and cracked, and down the crack of each of them showed a minute line of yellowish green, thrusting outward to meet the hot encouragement of the newly-risen sun. For a moment that was all, and then there stirred, and burst a third!

"It is seed," said Cavor. And then I heard him whisper very softly, "Life!"

"Life!" And immediately it poured upon us that our vast journey had not been made in vain, that we had come to no arid waste of minerals, but to a world that lived and moved! We watched intensely.[14]

Perhaps Bergonzi would want to claim a mythic content for such a vision; in any event, it seems that this redeemed, "artificial" landscape is still the ground of our latter-day universe. It is true that the First World War induced a very deep disconfirmation of the Edwardian Revelation, and that we have come to see that

> April is the cruellest month, breeding
> Lilacs out of the dead land . . .

but we still have a deep reverence for life itself. It might even be argued that Wells's account of life on the moon may be a new creation myth for post-Christian man, a moving beyond Darwinian crisis: "immediately it poured upon us that our vast journey had not been in vain, that we had come to no arid waste of minerals, but to a world that lived and moved!"

Bedford is so fascinated by the lunar scene that, as he relates, "I kept rubbing the glass before me with my sleeve, jealous of the faintest suspicion of mist"; the clarity of the scene is essential, and any subjectivity, any "impressionism," might suggest a reversion to the *fin-de-siècle* mode. Immediately before the passage (from *In the Days of the Comet*) that describes the "weedy, flowering barley field, that was in some way saturated with light and beauty," comes the section of the novel leading up to the "Change." Although this is a novel of 1906, it is not difficult to recognize the element of *fin-de-siècle* "mist." We are reminded of parts of *The Time Machine*:

[14] *The First Men in the Moon*, London, 1901, 87.

Someone pursued me, perhaps several people—I do not know, we left them all behind. . . .

We ran. For a space I was altogether intent upon the swift monotony of flight and pursuit. The sands were changed to a whirl of green moonshine, the air was thunder. A luminous green haze rolled about us. What did such things matter? We ran. Did I gain or lose? that was the question. They ran through a gap in a broken fence that sprang up abruptly out of the nothingness, and turned to the right. . . .

They were gone! Everything was going, but I kept on running. Once more I stumbled. There was something about my feet that impeded me, tall grass or heather, but I could not see what it was, only this smoke that eddied about my knees. There was a noise and spinning in my brain, a vain resistance to a dark green curtain that was falling, falling, falling, fold upon fold. Everything grew darker and darker. . . .

. . . all things ceased to be.

Here we are in Matthew Arnold's Victorian world where all is

> . . . turning, turning,
> In mazes of heat and sound.

But the comet induces a change which moves Leadford forward to a therapeutic renaissance:

I seemed to awaken out of a refreshing sleep. I did not awaken with a start, but opened my eyes, and lay very comfortably. . . .

I felt very light, full of the sense of physical well-being.

Following Bergonzi's suggestion about the earlier romances, we might here identify a neglected Edwardian myth of secular apocalypse. Just as the *fin-de-siècle* myths were not merely "fantasy," but reflected contemporary social and psychic conditions, so this Edwardian myth is not simply shallow Wellsian wish-fulfilment, but a vivid analogue of the actual process of psychic rebirth that seems to have occurred in the Edwardian period.

The primary strength of the work as model of centurial apocalypse is its principal weakness as a conventional novel. It has no simple sequential structure. The first half has close affinities with the ordinary suspense novel of the Victorian world, but just at the climax of the action, when the reader expects Leadford to murder Nettie and Verrall, the green mist falls. The speeded-up time of the murder-hunt makes the strongest possible contrast with the new order of time which follows the change. There is an effect similar to the truncated hunt at the end of William Golding's novel, *The Lord of the Flies.*[15]

The transition from a hysterically rapid process of uncontrolled violence to the redeemed springtime of a pastoral world is also the pattern of *The Winter's Tale*, whose structure is similarly split and "flawed." In each work an apocalyptic pastoralization occurs which provides the formal opportunity for measured discourse. In the second half of *In the Days of the Comet* a form of therapeutic society is constructed out of the ruins of the old order. This is typically Wellsian, of course, but in this particular novel the discursive element is presented in satisfying formal contrast to the strict sequentiality of the first section of the narrative. *In the Days of the Comet* is, then, an interesting attempt to render the transition to what I have called a Rieffian universe. The breakdown in linear, sequential narrative, and the breakthrough into a non-sequential narrative universe, reflects a general movement towards analytic activism. Wells uses an image strikingly similar to the "nihilistic" vision of the end of *Tono-Bungay*:

> We sat silently for a time before our vivisected passions.
> "Gods!" I cried, "and there was our poor little top-hamper of intelligence on all these waves of instinct and wordless desire, these foaming things of touch and sight and feeling, like—like a coop of hens washed overboard and clucking amidst the seas."
> Verrall laughed approval of the image I had struck out.
> "A week ago," he said, trying it further, "we were clinging to our chicken coops and going with the heave and pour. That was true enough a week ago. But today———?"
> "Today," I said, "the wind has fallen. The world storm is over. And each chicken coop has changed by a miracle to a vehicle that makes head against the sea." [16]

This concept of post-cultural man who escapes a purposeless clucking through cognitive control of himself and his environment is akin to Rieff's idea of a Freudian analytic therapy-for-therapy's-sake, in which the aim is to "keep going." In his

[15] London, 1955.
[16] *In the Days of the Comet*, 211.

para-Freudian assertion of the power of the ego and a concomitant passing beyond culture, Wells deliberately undermines the "cultural" content of his writing by using an image which is both banal and absurd. There is a built-in safeguard against the critic who might read such a passage and claim it to comprise a "myth of centurial apocalypse," say. By writing in this way Wells sets out to reverse the appeal being made to the reader as he reads the first part of the book. At first, such is the physiology of reading, the reader is bodily following Leadford on his murder-hunt; then Wells devalues all the emotional involvement of the reader by offering an absurd fiction of chickens and chicken coops. The reader is forced into an analytic mode in the very act of processing his own "literary" reactions, his fictional disappointments. The reader's vertigo is not least among the elements which come under cure when Wells deliberately destroys the cultural "integrity" of the novel, leaves the initial action unfinished, and proceeds to analyse the sexual relations between the characters with a patience which is unwittingly Freudian. Cultural ordering, which to Wells involves conforming to an evolved state of disinheritance and existing in perpetual crisis, is replaced by therapeutic community, involvement in the ongoing activist creation of a psychomorphous universe.

III

Kipps was published in 1905, a year before *In the Days of the Comet*, and presents a vision of England before change. Kipps himself comes to represent deprived existence badgered by the conditions of cultural order:

> The stupid little tragedies of these clipped and limited lives!
> As I think of them lying unhappily there in the darkness, my vision pierces the night. See what I can see! Above them, brooding over them, I tell you there is a monster, a lumpish monster, like some great griffin thing, like the Crystal Palace labyrinthodon, like Coote, like the leaden goddess of the Dunciad, like some fat, proud flunkey, like pride, like indolence, like all that is darkening and heavy and obstructive in life. It is matter and darkness, it is the anti-soul, it is the ruling power of this land, Stupidity. My Kippses live in its shadow. Shalford and his

apprenticeship system, the Hastings Academy, the ideas of Coote, the ideas of the old Kippses, all the ideas that have made Kipps what he is,—all these are a part of its shadow. But for that monster they might not be groping among false ideas to hurt one another so sorely; but for that, the glowing promise of childhood and youth might have had a happier fruition; thought might have awakened in them to meet the thought of the world, the quickening sunshine of literature pierced to the substance of their souls; their lives might not have been divorced, as now they are divorced, from the apprehension of beauty that we favoured ones are given,—the vision of the Grail that makes life fine for ever.[17]

Kipps's "clipped and limited" life is shown very much in class terms in the novel, but the total vision of the book is not directed by class-hostilities. The medical socialist's therapeutic imagination transcends matters of class, and turns for example to literature not for its 'cultural' embodiment of the finest values but for its "quickening sunshine" which "pierces" to the very "substance of . . . souls." The sentimental socialism of the passage continues:

I have laughed, and I laugh at these two people; I have sought to make you laugh. . . .

But I see through the darkness the souls of my Kippses as they are, as little pink strips of quivering living stuff, as things like the bodies of little, ill-nourished, ailing, ignorant children—children who feel pain, who are naughty and muddled and suffer, and do not understand why. And the claw of this Beast rests upon them.[18]

Wells's cry for better births and "a happier fruition" is fundamental to his therapeutic vision of cultural crisis. His dissociated existences, bemused by the cultural pressures which afflict them, constitute a means of defining a crisis in society. Even the "Story of a Simple Soul" can become a revolutionary realization of social fragmentation, in which the self's unwitting demands for therapy are the source of a transformative dynamic.

Wells refers to his design to make the reader laugh; in Kipps the comedy becomes the source of the reader's sympathy for the hero:

"And how does it feel to have twelve hundred a year?" asked

[17] *Kipps*, London, 1905, 392.
[18] 392-3.

Masterman, holding his cigarette to his nose tip in a curious manner.

"It's rum," confided Kipps, after a reflective interval. "It feels juiced rum." [19]

Masterman's unpleasant cynicism is the mark of revolution of the conventional kind. Kipps's innocuously inflated language, "clipping" and "limiting" as it is, establishes the implicit purity of Kipps's dissociated "soul" as a revolutionary instrument of a more radical kind.[20] Set into the world uttering absurdly anachronistic phrases, it undermines cultural coherence, making through its very vulnerability and imperfection the most compelling of requests for therapy. To Masterman accrues the guilt of putting such a therapeutic vision into words; but his vision is only an abstraction from Kipps's predicament, and depends upon implicit criteria of psychological well-being:

As for happiness, you want a world in order before money or property or any of those things have any real value, and this world, I tell you, is hopelessly out of joint. Man is a social animal with a mind nowadays that goes round the globe, and a community cannot be happy in one part and unhappy in another. It's all or nothing, no patching any more for ever. It is the standing mistake of the world not to understand that. Consequently people think there is a class or order somewhere just above them or just below them, or a country or place somewhere that is really safe and happy. . . . The fact is, Society is one body, and it is either well or ill. That's the law. This society we live in is ill. It's a fractious, feverish invalid, gouty, greedy, ill-nourished. You can't have a happy left leg with neuralgia, or a happy throat with a broken leg.[21]

We may note that cultural ordering, as in "a class or order" and "a country or place somewhere," is once again in Wells's thought replaced by therapeutic ordering. Happiness derives from a coherent "community" and "This society . . . is ill." The appeal of a therapeutic vision which partly derives its criteria of health from aesthetic considerations is clear in both the Beast passage and this speech of Masterman's. The words "ill-nourished," which appear in both passages, suggest existential deprivation.

[19] 288.
[20] There may be a parallel in this context between Kipps's "Simple Soul" and Stevie in Conrad's novel, *The Secret Agent*.
[21] 290.

But more than this, such words seem to be responding to a new kind of communal guilt or anxiety, foreshadowing the strange fascination that photographs of Biafran children have for us. In place of the Original Sin of the pre-Darwinian world, sickness, physical emaciation and "suffering" become the objects of redemption.

It is important to understand the primacy of the therapeutic motive in Wells's sensibility, and not to confuse the money-symbolism of *Kipps*, for example, with a thorough-going para-Marxism. As Masterman's speech suggests, Wells is not concerned with the historical importance of economic factors. Kipps is just as much involved with money at the end of the novel as at the beginning. But just as Ann's half of the sixpence is "redeemed," so is Kipps's money-dealing.

The symbolic structure of the novel seems simple. The divided sixpence represents the hygienic removal of a piece of "Muck"— as Chaffery calls coinage in *Love and Mr. Lewisham*[22]—and the substitution of individual human union between two people reinforcing the "worth" of the relationship. The sixpence when cut through is worthless as a coin, but is infinitely valuable, since it may symbolize mutual realization if the two halves are brought together again. The therapeutic process which works to still Kipps's alienated consciousness may be traced in two moments of the novel's development. When Kipps is in the dining-room of the Royal Grand Hotel, he is so out of place and so (as he fancies) laughed at in his attempts to eat "properly," that he undergoes a rapid adaptive change and finds himself emerging as a "Socialist":

> The mental change Kipps underwent was, in its way, what psychologists call a conversion. In a few moments all Kipps's ideals were changed. He who had been "practically a gentleman," the sedulous pupil of Coote, the punctilious raiser of hats, was instantly a rebel, an outcast, the hater of everything "stuck up," the foe of Society and the social order of today. Here they were among the profits of their robbery, these people who might do anything with the world. . . .
> "No thenks," he said to a dish.[23]

Wells catches admirably the funny-pathetic quality of the "foe of Society" who nevertheless makes an automatic effort to copy the

[22] London, 1900, 207.
[23] 306.

accents of "Society," and ultimately thereby to become Society. The scene is brought to life by the vividly idiosyncratic language which shows the dissociated existence of Kipps precariously adopting a cultural mode of being in the world. But from the extreme self-consciousness of his exposure in the dining-room, Kipps moves to an ultimate stilling of consciousness, where the word "reely" is a sign of existential authenticity, and where the unity of the family (Kipps, Ann and their child) is reflected in the final caught moment of union with natural beauty:

> Out of the darkness beneath the shallow weedy stream of his being rose a question, a question that looked up dimly and never reached the surface. It was the question of the wonder of the beauty, the purposeless, inconsecutive beauty, that falls so strangely among the happenings and memories of life. It never reached the surface of his mind, it never took to itself substance or form; it looked up merely as the phantom of a face might look, out of deep waters, and sank again into nothingness.
> "Artie," said Ann.
> He woke up and pulled a stroke. "What?" he said.
> "Penny for your thoughts, Artie."
> "I reely don't think I was thinking of anything," he said at last, with a smile. "No." [24]

In this priceless unconscious union with the universe (valued ironically at a penny) there is a kind of harmony and sense of well-being not previously depicted in Wells's novels. It is the harmony of the post-cultural self in intimate, mutually realizing relations with another self, the harmony of "cosmic" existence. Such a harmony is available to Kipps only after he has found it possible to give up all "cultural" pretensions, only after he and his family have established an intensely private bridge-head beyond culture.

IV

Tono-Bungay is less conventional in structure than *Kipps*, and it may be that recent accounts of the novel [25] have concerned

[24] 424–5.
[25] Notably in Kenneth B. Newell, "The Structure of H. G. Wells's

themselves too exclusively with structural considerations. The apparently uncontrolled alternation of sexual and socioeconomic episodes in *Tono-Bungay* might be interpreted as an analytic process for relating the Freudian and Marxist predicaments in an ongoing way, the activist remedy that Wells recommends at the end of the novel being implemented in the actual "anarchic" sequence of events in the novel. The very gap or aesthetic discrepancy between the sexual and social themes is in itself, in this view, the grounds for the establishing of a remedial Freudo-Marxist dialectic. The image of individual man "making and passing," "striving upon a hidden mission, out to the open sea," [26] is not superadded to the novel, nor is it conflicting in spirit with the analytic-agnostic attitude implicit in the ordering of the material of the novel.

Structural approaches to *Tono-Bungay* are, in this view, rather wide of the critical mark. It is a novel which defines itself as it proceeds as an ongoing process; it would be proper to talk not of its structure, but of the experience it engenders during the time the reader spends reading it. The form of *Tono-Bungay* analogizes Edwardian crisis temporally. Whereas the great Victorian novels move always towards an end, *Tono-Bungay* is structured around the release of the narrator from an ending process. At the end "through the confusion sounds another note," [27] and there is discernible "a music beneath the noise." [28] At first sight the narrator's opting out of contemporary decadence, and submission to historical process, may seem Marxist. But it may be a mistake to dwell on the Marxist character of Wells's Utopianization, for that Utopianization is both technological and at the same time intensely private. Wells grew more and more convinced of the programmatic need for self-submission to human

---

Tono-Bungay," *English Fiction in Transition*, iv (1961) 1–8; Laurence Poston, "*Tono-Bungay*: Wells's Unconstructed Tale," *College English*, xxvi (1965), 433–8; David Lodge, "*Tono-Bungay* and the Condition of England," *The Language of Fiction*, London, 1966, 214–42; Bernard Bergonzi, Introduction, *Tono-Bungay*, Boston, Mass., 1966, v–xxviii; Richard H. Costa, "H. G. Wells's" *Tono-Bungay*: "Review of New Studies," *English Literature in Transition*, x (1967), 89–96.

[26] The last lines of the novel, London, (1909), 493.

[27] *Tono-Bungay*, London, 1908, 491.

[28] Bliss Carman, *The Making of Personality*, London, 1908, v.

racial process, but his later theorizing should not be allowed to distort our view of the Edwardian novels, which are novels of private consciousness, and make demands which are fundamentally existential.

In *Tono-Bungay* Wells's "nihilistic" faith in the destroyer, "X_2," represents the denial of any cultural teleology, the Marxist included. The novelistic registration of the other note which sounds through confusion is the sense of redeemed private time in the modulation of tenses in the penultimate paragraph of the novel:

> Though, as a matter of fact, X_2 isn't intended for the empire, or indeed for the hands of any European power. We offered it to our people first, but they would have nothing to do with me, and I have long since ceased to trouble much about such questions. I have come to see myself from the outside, my country from the outside—without illusion. We make and pass.[29]

The final present tense represents a temporal freeing similar to the freeing at the end of *Mr. Polly*, a freeing from the very apocalyptic sense which has been responsible for the panicky, Mailerian structuring of events in the novel in the trajectile form. In a sense the novel depicts the process of apocalyptic Utopianization which is undertaken by all men who move beyond culture into the existential mode; the movement in *Tono-Bungay* would seem to work towards a privatism in which the Utopian rewards include immediate release from the pressures of an unknown future. The achieved mode is no mere "living for the present," but involves the responsible and constant commitment of the individual to an ongoing cognitive process.

The conventional reading of *Tono-Bungay* raises this problem: at the beginning of the novel the narrator admits himself to be in urgent need of self-expression, and he acknowledges the disorder of the material he will be assembling; at the end of the novel the narrator makes large claims for a mature attitude and a settled attitude, but doesn't seem to remember that the very act of writing the novel has itself been a self-professed therapy—he seems to attribute the therapeutic process to his actual experiences and not to the confessional telling of them in the novel. The

[29] *Tono-Bungay*, 492-3.

reader, absorbed in the novel as cognitive process, does not necessarily, however, find this a major difficulty; the events of consciousness implicit in the first-person ordering of the story are the events which consolidate the feeling of a final redemption from cultural time. When Wells begins the book he uses his narrator to take the reader with him into a world of cultural crisis, where no assured moral response is possible:

> I want to set out my own queer love experiences too, such as they are, for they troubled and distressed and swayed me hugely, and they still seem to contain all sorts of irrational and debatable elements that I shall be the clearer-headed for getting on paper.[30]

When George Ponderevo claims at the end of the novel to be "clearer-headed" and seems to forget that the writing out of the novel has itself effected the cure, the apparent lack of novelistic tact is positively useful in that it establishes the revolutionary nature of the analytic process. By the end of the novel the reader has learned to make do without the reassurance of a conventional end-oriented narrative; he has learned to live beyond the "cultural" ordering which the narrator diagnoses as the source of the initial confusion. George Ponderevo finally goes beyond conventional "community" and enters the negative community of private selves redeemed by technological process. His revolution is similar to that described by Philip Rieff:

> . . . the modern cultural revolution has built into itself a unique prophylaxis: it is deliberately not in the name of any new order of communal purpose that it is taking place. On the contrary, this revolution is being fought for a permanent disestablishment of any deeply internalized moral demands, in a world which can guarantee a plenitude produced without reference to the rigid maintenance of any particular interdictory system.[31]

Tono-Bungay is the remarkable *tour de force* that it is for the very reason that it engenders cultural disintegration in the reader's experience of reading the novel. By the end of the novel the reader is able more nearly to share the experience of "post-cultural" man, because he has been sharing in the process by which a confused mind has set out, analytically, the grounds of its confusion:

[30] 6.
[31] *The Triumph of the Therapeutic*, London, 1966.

> I remember how I laughed aloud at the glimpse of the name of a London County Council steamboat that ran across me. *Caxton* it was called, and another was *Pepys* and another was *Shakespeare*. They seemed so wildly out of place, splashing about in that confusion. One wanted to take them out and wipe them and put them back in some English gentleman's library.[32]

And if he has read sensitively he will feel the need for the implementation of therapy:

> To my mind radio-activity is a real disease of matter. Moreover it is a contagious disease. It spreads. . . . It is in matter exactly what the decay of our old culture is in society, a loss of traditions and distinctions and assured reactions.[33]

The passing of the "old cultural" mode of social organization (where reactions were semi-automatic and "assured") is the signal for the initiation of a therapeutic vision as outlined in the final paragraphs of the novel. The effect that "quap" has upon nearby human beings is to make them experience the kind of neurotic symptoms from which Mr. Polly suffers at the beginning of the later novel:

> I believe that the primary influence of the quap upon us was to increase the conductivity of our nerves, but that is a mere unjustifiable speculation on my part. At any rate it gave a sort of east wind effect to life. We all became irritable, clumsy, languid, and disposed to be impatient with our languor.[34]

In *The History of Mr. Polly* Wells asks: "Why cannot doctors give us an antidote to the east wind? " [35] By the end of *Tono-Bungay* the set of the reader's cultural expectations has been so disconfirmed, his need for "structure" and end-orientation has been so neglected, and his own moral insufficiency has been brought home to him that he may be pleased to leave the public confusion of culture and enter with Wells the cold and intensely private world of his therapeutic activism. "Psychiatrically," as R. D. Laing has said in another context, "this would appear as ex-patients helping future patients to go mad." [36]

[32] 489.
[33] 413.
[34] 415.
[35] London, 1909, 12.
[36] *The Politics of Experience*, Harmondsworth, Middx., 1967, 106.

V

The History of Mr. Polly sets out more conventionally the cognitive
process which permits its hero to proceed beyond the moral
ordering of his life towards a mode which might be described as
existential. Mr. Polly's arson and attempted suicide are cognitive
acts, "mad" in terms of internalized cultural values, but ultimately equivalent to an active mode of enlightenment. As Wells
writes in a well-known passage:

> But when a man has once broken through the paper walls of
> everyday circumstance, those unsubstantial walls that hold so
> many of us securely prisoned from the cradle to the grave, he has
> made a discovery. If the world does not please you, *you can change
> it.* Determine to alter it at any price, and you can change it
> altogether.[37]

In place of the conformative *fin-de-sièclism* of *The Wheels of
Chance*,[38] for example, which is content to remain largely in the
symptomatic mode, this later novel traces a therapeutic pattern
of development in its comic hero, and activist cognition is
specifically depicted as a therapeutic process. The book starts
with Mr. Polly suffering from indigestion and "sick of everything," [39] unable to diagnose his general malaise: "He suffered
from indigestion now nearly every afternoon in his life, but as he
lacked introspection he projected the associated discomfort upon
the world" (p. 7). After the fire at Fishbourne, however, his
symptomatic condition emerges more clearly, and a suitable
alloplastic therapy is formulated:

> There are no circumstances in the world that determined action
> cannot alter, unless perhaps they are the walls of a prison cell,
> and even those will dissolve and change, I am told, into the
> infirmary compartment, at any rate, for the man who can fast
> with resolution. I give these things as facts and information, and
> with no moral intimations. And Mr. Polly, lying awake at nights,

[37] *The History of Mr. Polly*, London, 1910, 283.
[38] London, 1896.
[39] London, 1910, 7. Further references to this book are put in parentheses in
the text.

with a renewed indigestion, with Miriam sleeping sonorously beside him, and a general air of inevitableness about his situation, saw through it, understood his former despair (pp. 283–4).

The moralistic, legalistic prison-walls of cultural circumstance "dissolve" into the walls of the infirmary; we move beyond "moral intimations" to cognition, to "seeing through." Mr. Polly sees himself for the first time as involved in a process of self-cure.

At the end of the novel Polly's cure is complete, and the process is specified as therapeutic, even medical, by a reference back to the hero's initial state of health:

> One summer afternoon, about five years after his first coming to the Potwell Inn, Mr. Polly found himself sitting under the pollard willow, fishing for dace. It was a plumper, browner, and healthier Mr. Polly altogether than the miserable bankrupt with whose dyspeptic portrait our novel opened. He was fat, but with a fatness more generally diffused, and the lower part of his face was touched to gravity by a small square beard (p. 355).

The comedy may hide the fact that Mr. Polly is a strikingly new type in English fiction. His final achievement (when he has come to benefit from the good things of life at the Potwell Inn) is close to that of Rieffian revolution:

> . . . this revolution is being fought for a permanent disestablishment of any deeply internalized moral demand, in a world which can guarantee a plenitude produced without reference to the rigid maintenance of any particular interdictory system.[40]

In a sense he is a Romantic hero, but he is post-Romantic in the transformative nature of his refusal to undertake the self-deprivation upon which culture must depend:

> I have failed in presenting Mr. Polly altogether if I have not made you see that he was in many respects an artless child of Nature, far more untrained, undisciplined, and spontaneous than an ordinary savage. And he was really glad, for all that little drawback of fear, that he had had the courage to set fire to his house, and fly, and come to the Potwell Inn (p. 357).

The pre-requisite for a "permissive society" in this context seems to be a human type recognizable for its dissociation from cultural

[40] *The Triumph of the Therapeutic*, London, 1966, 239–40.

modes of adaptation. Only such a subject, "more untrained" and "undisciplined" than a savage whose life is "clipped" and "limited" by cultural loyalties, can fulfil the promise of therapeutic activism.

The post-cultural self in the *fin-de-siècle* myth lives in a Godless universe, attenuated, flickering in a limbo of transition. The hollow universe and hollow self, and the images of emaciation and deprivation which are pervasive in 1890s literature, become polarized after 1900 into an opposite mode. The Edwardian typology as manifest in Mr. Polly bears the same relation to *fin-de-siècle* man as the later Polly bears to the earlier:

> It was a plumper, browner, and healthier Mr. Polly altogether than the miserable bankrupt with whose dyspeptic portrait our novel opened (p. 355).

By a striking reversal, the empty clothes of the Invisible Man are replaced by a Mr. Polly who is "fat, but with a fatness more generally diffused" (p. 355). If we return to J. Hillis Miller's version of Darwinian crisis, we shall see how closely Mr. Polly's cure matches the symptoms of late-Victorian crisis:

> When God is annihilated, at the same time man annihilates himself and annihilates also the world around him. He annihilates them in the sense of hollowing them out, emptying them of any substantial presence. Human subjectivity comes more and more to be experienced as a lack, as a devouring emptiness, as an unassuageable hunger for some lost plenitude of being.[41]

The teleological and cultural deprivation and the devaluation of all values implicit in *fin-de-siècle* crisis become in the Edwardian revolution the very grounds for the implementation of the new therapy (". . . this revolution is being fought for a permanent disestablishment of any deeply internalized moral demands"). And the late-Victorian nostalgia for "some lost plenitude of being" becomes the basis for the Edwardian Utopianization of reality which "can guarantee a plenitude produced without reference to the rigid maintenance of any particular interdictory system."

"Plenitude" is perhaps the primary theme of the final chapter of *The History of Mr. Polly*, in which the words "the fat woman"

[41] *The Form of Victorian Fiction*, Notre Dame, Ind., 1968, 32.

occur fourteen times in the seven pages. In place of *fin-de-siècle* depletion ("We need to put a living soul in the clothed body"), Wells presents an image of repletion:

> Mr. Polly sat beside the fat woman at one of the little green tables at the back of the Potwell Inn, and struggled with the mystery of life. It was one of those evenings serenely luminous, amply and atmospherically still, when the river bend was at its best. A swan floated against the dark green masses of the further bank, the stream flowed broad and shining to its destiny, with scarce a ripple—except where the reeds came out from the headland, and the three poplars rose clear and harmonious against the sky of green and yellow. It was as if everything lay securely within a great, warm, friendly globe of crystal sky. It was as safe and enclosed and fearless as a child that has still to be born. It was an evening full of the quality of tranquil, unqualified assurance. Mr. Polly's mind was filled with the persuasion that indeed all things whatsoever must needs be satisfying and complete (p. 368).

"Some things I can't believe," says Mr. Polly to the fat woman, "and one is your being a skeleton" (p. 373).

But if Mr. Polly's cure foreshadows our own Rieffian therapy, there are other elements in the novel which are directly opposed to the Rieffian mode. If Polly's activism corresponds to a cognitive existential therapy, there are moments when Wells seems to be recommending an adjustive therapy or a therapy centred in society itself:

> He could not grasp what was wrong with him. He made enormous efforts to diagnose his case. . . . for all his attempts at self-reproach and self-discipline he felt at bottom that he wasn't at fault.
>
> As a matter of fact all the elements of his troubles had been adequately diagnosed by a certain high-browed, spectacled gentleman living at Highbury, wearing a gold pince-nez, and writing for the most part in the beautiful library of the Climax Club. This gentleman did not know Mr. Polly personally, but he had dealt with him generally as "one of those ill-adjusted units that abound in a society that has failed to develop a collective intelligence and a collective will for order commensurate with its perplexities" (pp. 75–6).

And if this seems ironically distanced and not necessarily corresponding with the narrator's own beliefs, there is further evidence in Chapter 10 of the novel:

> If our community was collectively anything more than a feeble
> idiot, it would burn most of London and Chicago, for example,
> and build sane and beautiful cities in the place of these
> pestilential heaps of private property (p. 357).

What Wells is missing in these discursive passages is the fact that
this very societal failure "to develop a collective intelligence and
a collective will for order" is the basis of Polly's intensely private
Utopianization of experience. His quasi-nihilistic activism derives directly from the lack within him of any cultural allegiance.
His determination to fight off Uncle Jim and to defend the world
he has created by discovering, is atheoretical and works simply
towards sustaining "a plenitude of being." More and more after
1910 these discursive passages tend to take over from the truly
fictional element in Wells's work, and the Rieffian, para-Freudian therapies of the Edwardian fiction are replaced by a
commitment therapy directed towards the institution of a variety
of global entities, including the "World State," the "World
Brain" and the "World Mind."

VI

Kipps and Polly, though appearing in books which sporadically
recommend societal commitment therapies, extend the Dickensian consolidation of the self to the extreme point of Rieffian
privatism. Though ostensibly founded upon a Socialist theory of
the perniciousness of private property, they promote a mode
of self-possession which is nowadays implicit in the plasticity of
property and the affluence and plenitude of Western life. The
private linguistic worlds of Dickens's characters are well known;
they might be more clearly understood if we took note of the
perception that Mr. Polly "has a strange fantastic culture of his
own." [42] Deprived of access to a common societal source of
cultural order, the self adopts its own parodic behaviour patterns.
Mr. Polly admits that he has always been the "skeptaceous sort"
(p. 370), and his distortion of language betrays his determination
to exist on his own terms. He becomes the centre of "culture" in

[42] "Notes on Nelson's New Novels," appended to *The History of Mr. Polly*,
London, 1910.

the universe, and his decisions are existential decisions, not at all dictated by internalized moral standards. His language revolutionizes reality as defined linguistically; its transformative function may be compared with the conformative language of Uncle Jim. The latter's mythically frightening quality may in part derive from his loyalty to a primitive cultural mode:

> "Bolls!" came the thick voice of the enemy behind him, as one who accepts a challenge, and, bleeding but indomitable, Uncle Jim entered the house.
> "Bolls!" he said, surveying the bar. "Fightin' with bolls! I'll showim fightin' with bolls!" (pp. 326–7).

Distortion of language here is an act of cultural violence, a subscription to the "clipped" and "limited" behaviour patterns peculiar to a definite group of people. There is no appeal to such a creature's "higher qualities," since all the values implicit in his behaviour are registered in the conformity of his language to its lower-class pattern. The battle at the Potwell Inn then becomes a Darwinian fight for survival between cultural and post-cultural man. Polly wins because he is not limited to any kind of "savage" culture; he ignores Uncle Jim's protestations that ducking him in the water "ain't fair fightin' " (p. 332). Polly's privatism is well adapted to 'the private war.'

Uncle Jim may remind us of the wretched animals vivisected into semi-humans by Dr. Moreau[43] and suffering the cultural fettering defined by Nietzsche:

> Man, imprisoned in an iron cage of errors, became a caricature of man, sick, wretched, ill-disposed toward himself, full of hatred for the impulses of life, full of mistrust of all that is beautiful and happy in life, a walking picture of misery.[44]

Such a cultural fettering is, in fact, the essence of Wells's definition of Leadford, Kipps and Polly before the respective "Changes" that alter their lives. Our own sense of the power of the myth of well-being may ultimately derive from the disgust which Nietzschean, "sick," "imprisoned" man instigated in so many Edwardian sensibilities.

[43] See *The Island of Dr. Moreau*, London, 1896.
[44] *The Will to Power*, translated by Walter Kaufmann and R. J. Hollingdale, London, 1968, 214.

Tono-Bungay

and the Condition of England

by David Lodge

The famous quarrel between Henry James and H. G. Wells, so ably documented by Leon Edel and Gordon N. Ray,[1] takes on, in the critic's contemplation of it, an almost allegorical quality. It was a classic encounter between a great theorist and exponent of the aesthetically "pure," modern, international novel, and a redoubtable spokesman for and practitioner of the rambling, discursive, aesthetically "impure" novel of the traditional English type. At the time of their breach Wells must have seemed the victor, for he was riding the wave of popular acclaim, while the 'major phase' of James was misunderstood and neglected. Time and changing literary taste have brought about a reversal of this situation; now it is Wells who is neglected and even despised, while James sits in glory on Parnassus. Just recently this movement of the scales has been checked by a renewal of interest in Wells's early scientific romances, an interest promoted particularly by Bernard Bergonzi's excellent study *The Early H. G. Wells* (Manchester, 1961). But most modern critics would still endorse Mark Schorer's words: "as James grows for us . . . Wells disappears." [2]

The Edel-Ray book can only confirm this process. On the

"*Tono-Bungay* and the Condition of England." From David Lodge, *Language of Fiction* (London: Routledge & Kegan Paul Ltd. and New York: Columbia University Press, 1966). Copyright © 1966 by David Lodge. Reprinted by permission of the author and publishers.

[1] *Henry James and H. G. Wells: A Record of their Friendship, their Debate on the Art of Fiction, and their Quarrel*, edited with an introduction by Leon Edel and Gordon N. Ray (London, 1958).

[2] Mark Schorer, "Technique as Discovery," *Critiques and Essays on Modern Fiction 1920–1951*, ed. John W. Aldridge (New York, 1952), p. 72.

purely human level, James probably emerges with more credit; and he certainly has the best of the literary debate. The eloquence of his *credo* in the final letter, "It is art that *makes* life, makes interest, makes importance, for our consideration and application of these things, and I know of no substitute whatever for the force and beauty of its process" [3]—is overwhelming. However, as in most literary quarrels, James and Wells were too involved in their own literary destinies to do each other justice; and Wells was plainly irritated by James's mandarin gestures into doing *himself* injustice, affecting a literary barbarism which the skill of his own work belies.

I am not going to argue that Wells was as great a novelist as James, but I am going to argue that *Tono-Bungay* (1909) is a much better novel than it is commonly supposed to be. Clearly, we shall never reach this conclusion if we read the novel as we read a novel by James, in the way James has taught us to read him, and to read other novelists. *Tono-Bungay* sins, deliberately, against most of the Jamesian commandments: it is picaresque, full of apparent digressions in the form both of episodes, and of expository comment on politics, economics, history, and society. It is told in the first person, and rejoices in "the terrible *fluidity* of self-revelation" [4] which James saw as the great weakness of that mode of narration. Its characters are largely of the "flat," humorous variety. Plainly, *Tono-Bungay* will not offer the same satisfactions as *The Ambassadors*. But I suggest that if we read *Tono-Bungay* with an open mind, with attention to its language, to the passages where that language becomes most charged with imaginative energy, we shall find that it is an impressive, and certainly coherent, work of art.

At first sight, this may seem a surprising recommendation, because insensitivity to language is one of the commonest complaints made by critics of Wells. In the essay in which he calls for closer attention to language in novel-criticism, Mark Schorer invokes Wells as an example of a novelist whose severe limitations will be exposed by such an approach.[5] Norman

[3] James and Wells, *op. cit.*, p. 267.
[4] Preface to *The Ambassadors*, *The Art of the Novel*, ed. R. P. Blackmur (New York, 1935), p. 321.
[5] Schorer, *op cit.*, p. 71 ff.

Nicholson says, "as for style, he had none, if by style we mean the shaping of sentences which will be a pleasure in themselves." [6] Vincent Brome says, "words were not weighed and flavoured with care in *Tono-Bungay*." [7] Arnold Kettle says:

> Wells himself achieved in his novels no satisfactory artistic expression of his own vision of life. Part of the trouble would seem to be in his incurably slap-dash, slip-shod method of composition. He does not give himself time to search for the right word, let alone organize his total material.[8]

There is a certain amount of truth in these criticisms, but the weight they should be given in assessing the novel needs to be carefully measured. One can certainly find scattered through *Tono-Bungay* examples of loose grammar and careless punctuation which obscure meaning and serve no perceptible expressive function. But such faults—although they remain faults—cause less disturbance than they would in a novel by, for example, James, because Wells's undertaking in *Tono-Bungay* does not require the elegant, harmonious, intricate kind of language adopted by James, but a language that is hurried, urgent, groping. This is not to say that we can ever excuse "bad" writing—writing that consistently fails to meet the legitimate expectations of the reader. But such expectations must arise out of the novel itself.

More than "style," in Nicholson's sense, is at stake here. Kettle, for instance, complains that Wells fails "to people adequately the world of the novel. There are almost no characters in *Tono-Bungay* who grip the imagination of the reader." [9] But what if Wells set out to grip the imagination of the reader in other ways? This, after all, was the point at issue between him and James:

> The important thing which I tried to argue with Henry James was that the novel of completely consistent characterisation, arranged beautifully in a strong and rounded story, and painted deep and round, no more exhausts the possibilities of the novel,

[6] Norman Nicholson, *H. G. Wells* (London, 1950), p. 98.

[7] Vincent Brome, *H. G. Wells: a Biography* (London, 1951), p. 108.

[8] Arnold Kettle, *An Introduction to the English Novel*, Vol. II (Grey Arrow paperback edition, 1962), p. 94.

[9] *Ibid.*, p. 95.

than the art of Velasquez exhausts the possibilities of the painted picture.[10]

But if *Tono-Bungay* is not a novel of the Jamesian type, of what type is it? It is confessional in form. "I want to tell—*myself*" says the narrator, George Ponderevo, at the outset; but adds immediately: "and my impressions of the thing as a whole, to say things I have come to feel intensely of the laws, traditions, usages and ideas we call society" (I, i, 2). He feels qualified to do so because his career has led him through an "extensive cross-section of the British social organism" (I, i, 1).

The Victorians had a name for this kind of undertaking in fiction: the "Condition of England novel." This description was often applied to novels which sought to articulate and interpret, in the mode of fiction, the changing nature of English society in an era of economic, political, religious, and philosophical revolution. In *Coningsby* (1844) Disraeli refers to "that Condition of England question, of which our generation hears so much." [11] Other novels of this type include Disraeli's own *Sybil* (1845), Mrs. Gaskell's *Mary Barton* (1848), and *North and South* (1855), Dickens's *Hard Times* (1854), Charles Kingsley's *Alton Locke* (1850), and *Yeast* (1851), and George Eliot's *Felix Holt* (1866). And there were a host of justly-forgotten minor novels in the *genre*. The central issue for most of these writers was the economic one. Carlyle begins his *Past and Present* (1843):

> The condition of England question, on which many pamphlets are now in the course of publication, and many thoughts unpublished are going on in every reflective head, is justly regarded as one of the most ominous, and withal one of the strangest, ever seen in this world. England is full of wealth, of multifarious produce, supply for human want in every kind; yet England is dying of inanition.[12]

The voice of Carlyle reminds us however, that the condition of England question was not merely an economic one, but part of the continuous cultural debate about the place of human values in a society given over to materialism, a debate which has been sustained from the Industrial revolution to the present day, and

---

[10] Wells, *Experiment in Autobiography* (London, 1934), p. 493.

[11] Disraeli, *Coningsby*, Book II, Chapter 1.

[12] *Past and Present* (Everyman edition, 1912), p. 1.

which has been so well surveyed by Raymond Williams in *Culture and Society.* Not only is the question still alive for Wells's generation—the very phrase is still alive. And the phrase is important: it invites us to consider England as a social organism whose health is suspect, which, as I shall try to show, is precisely Wells's perspective in *Tono-Bungay.* In the very same year that *Tono-Bungay* appeared (1909), C. F. G. Masterman* published *The Condition of England,* a book of social criticism in the tradition of Carlyle and Arnold, which it is fascinating to read in conjunction with *Tono-Bungay.* Masterman had read the page proofs of Wells's novel while preparing his own book,[13] and clearly he was very excited by it, for he frequently alludes to it.

"The hero of [Wells's] greatest novel," says Masterman, "reveals an experience fragmentary and disconnected in a tumultuous world." [14] With this may be coupled a passage from Wells's *An Experiment in Autobiography,* in which Wells argues that the fact that the English novel matured at a time of social fixity inevitably tilted the novelist's interests in the direction of individual characters reacting and conflicting within a comfortably stable social framework. He says that the novel's "standards were established within that apparently permanent frame and the criticism of it began to be irritated and perplexed when, through a new instability, the splintering frame began to get into the picture." [15] Wells's literary history, as is often the case with practising writers, is somewhat over-dramatized by his own sense of artistic purpose: Wells was not as revolutionary as he thought. But the comment yields an important clue to the understanding of *Tono-Bungay.* For here the frame does get into the picture; one might almost say the frame *is* the picture. That is, the main vehicle of Wells's social analysis of the condition of England in *Tono-Bungay* is not the story or the characters, but the descriptive commentary which, in most novels, we regard as the frame. I

---

* C. F. G. Masterman was born in 1873 and died in 1923. He was a Junior Minister in Asquith's 1908 Government, and subsequently held a series of other important political posts. He was a journalist, and had many contacts with the radical literary world.

[13] C. F. G. Masterman, *The Condition of England,* ed. J. T. Boulton (London, 1960), p. xiv.

[14] *Ibid.,* p. 181.

[15] Wells, *op. cit.,* p. 494.

refer to the descriptions of landscape and townscape, of architecture and domestic interiors, and the narrator's reflection on them, which occupy so prominent a place in the novel.

The function of these descriptions seems to me different from the function of description in other novels discussed in this book—different from Charlotte Brontë's real and visionary landscapes, different from Hardy's double-sided Nature, different from James's Paris. It comes closest to Dickens's Coketown, as we might expect, for that is the setting of another Condition of England novel. But Coketown *is* a setting, a "frame." The England of *Tono-Bungay* is not merely an appropriate setting for the gestures of Wells's characters, not merely a means of symbolizing their inner lives—not, in other words, something which gets its meaning from the individual lives which inhabit it. It is simply the central character of the novel, as England is the central character of Shakespeare's history plays.

A summary of Wells's diagnosis of the Condition of England in *Tono-Bungay* might be formulated as follows: Late Victorian and Edwardian England is a country dedicated to aimlessness and waste. The social and political principles of 1688 have not been replaced by any new theories, although society has been economically transformed by the Industrial Revolution. Consequently, capitalism has been allowed to burgeon without control, creating "the most unpremeditated, subtle, successful, and aimless plutocracy that ever encumbered the destinies of mankind" (III, ii, 7); and forcing the mass of mankind into living conditions of barbarous dreariness. If things continue to drift in this way, they can only get worse.

This pessimistic analysis of the Condition of England is conveyed partly in the main narrative line, which concerns the rise of Edward Ponderevo, George's uncle, to the financial heights, and his abrupt collapse into bankruptcy and dishonour. It is an effective parable of modern capitalism, but it is not the organizing principle in the design of *Tono-Bungay*. Nor are the episodes in George's life which are unrelated to his uncle and which mainly concern the unsatisfactory nature of his relationships with women. The organizing principle of *Tono-Bungay* is to be found in the web of description and commentary by which all the proliferating events and characters of the story are placed in a comprehensive political, social, and historical perspective. In the characteristic manner of the novelist, Wells develops this role of description out of the routine devices of concrete particularity and specificity. Houses, rooms, furnishings, townscapes, landscapes, and landscaped landscapes, are observed and described with a shrewd eye, placing the characters in a recognizable realistic environment, and serving as indices of their social status, tastes, and temperaments. But the language of the novel, like Dickens's language for Coketown, invests these inanimate objects and collections of objects with a strange and sinister life of their own, more powerful than the life of any individual character. It is, however, a diseased life. Running through the whole novel there is a strain of disease and decay imagery which establishes its theme and draws the episodic narrative into a coherent design. Seen in this perspective, the fact that "Tono-Bungay," the foundation of Ponderevo's immense fortune, should be a quack *medicine*, which falsely claims to cure all the ills of modern society, from boredom, fatigue, and strain, to falling hair and ageing gums, has a more than fortuitous appropriateness; George's failure to achieve a satisfactory and mature sexual relationship becomes a symptom of the universal disorder ("Love," he says, "like everything else in this immense process of social disorganization in which we live, is a thing adrift, a fruitless thing broken away from its connections" (IV, ii, 2)); and the "quap" episode, which many critics have taken to be an afterthought designed merely to give a flagging story a lift, earns its place in the novel as a logical, though daring piece of symbolic action.

It is the language of the novel which binds it into a unified whole, setting up verbal echoes which establish connections between the many disparate subjects of George's discourse, and giving that discourse a consistent and individual tone of voice. To summarize: George sees life in terms of society, and society as an *organism* or *system* which is often spatially conceived in terms of architecture or topography, and which is involved in a *process* of *change* and *growth* characterized by negative qualities of *confusion*, *disorder*, *disarrangement*, *disturbance*, *degeneration*, *dissolution*, *disproportion*, *muddle*, and *waste*, and more concretely, by *cancer*, *disease*, *decay*, *festering*, *swelling*, and *rot*. The spectacle is *huge*, *immense*, *stupendous*—hence all the more *strange* and *sinister*. These words, or words with associated meanings, recur in the most heightened passages of the novel, and suggest that Wells used language with more discrimination and a firmer sense of artistic purpose and design than critics have usually given him credit for.

Clearly, however, Wells's undertaking in *Tono-Bungay* is not compatible with the canons of the aesthetically pure and symmetrical novel; and he takes steps to deflect an appeal to such canons in the prefatory remarks of his narrator. Indeed, Wells seems to be rehearsing his debate with James in such passages as these:

> I warn you that this book is going to be something of an agglomeration. I want to trace my social trajectory (and my uncle's) as the main line of my story, but as this is my first novel and almost certainly my last, I want to get in, too, all sorts of things that struck me, things that amused me and impressions I got—even though they don't minister directly to my narrative at all. . . . My ideas of a novel all through are comprehensive rather than austere. (I, i, 1)
>
> I've read an average share of novels and made some starts before this beginning, and I've found the restraints and rules of the art (as I made them out) impossible for me. . . . I fail to see how I can be other than a lax, undisciplined story-teller. I must sprawl and flounder, comment and theorise, if I am to get the thing out I have in mind. (I, i, 2)

This is not an admission of failure on Wells's part, but a rhetorical device to prepare the reader for the kind of novel *Tono-Bungay* is—a case of artlessness concealing art. The major technical problem confronting the Condition of England novelist—as nineteenth-century examples show—is how to accommodate within an imaginative structure an abundance of material of a kind which is usually treated discursively. Wells's solution is to use a narrator who asserts at the outset his intention of commenting, describing, and theorizing, and to invest his most powerful literary resources in this area of the novel.

George Ponderevo begins his chronicle, in the conventional way, with an account of his boyhood and early impressions "in the shadow of Bladesover House,' Lady Drew's stately home, where his mother was employed as a housekeeper.

> Bladesover lies up on the Kentish Downs, eight miles perhaps from Ashborough; and its old pavilion, a little wooden parody of

the temple of Vesta at Tibur, upon the hill-crest behind the house, commands in theory at least a view of either sea, of the Channel southward and the Thames to the north-east. The park is the second largest in Kent, finely wooded with well-placed beeches, many elms and some sweet chestnuts, abounding in little valleys and hollows of bracken, with springs and a stream and three fine ponds and multitudes of fallow deer. The house was built in the eighteenth century, it is of pale red brick in the style of a French chateau, and save for one pass among the crests which opens to blue distances, to minute, remote, oast-set farm-houses and copses and wheatfields and the occasional gleam of water, its hundred and seventeen windows look on nothing but its own wide and handsome territories. A semi-circular screen of great beeches masks the church and village, which cluster picturesquely about the highroad along the skirts of the great park. (I, i, 3)

This seems a fairly unexceptional descriptive set-piece. But, apart from the faintly ironic and decidedly unawed tone of the narrator ("parody," "in theory") the detail of the windows, the self-regarding eyes of Bladesover, placed in an emphatic position at the end of a long sentence, and the noting of the careful concealment from these eyes of the lesser buildings dependent upon Bladesover, suggest that the scene has a more than pictorial significance. This becomes explicit in the next paragraph:

Now, the unavoidable suggestion of that wide park and that fair large house, dominating church, village and the country-side, was that they represented the thing that mattered supremely in the world, and that all other things had significance only in relation to them. They represented the Gentry, the Quality, by and through and for whom the rest of the world, the farming folk, and the labouring folk, the tradespeople of Ashborough and the upper servants and the lower servants and the servants of the estate, breathed and lived and were permitted. And the Quality did it so quietly and thoroughly, the great house mingled so solidly and effectually with earth and sky, the contrast of its spacious hall and saloon and galleries, its airy housekeeper's room and warren of offices with the meagre dignities of the vicar, and the pinched and stuffy rooms of even the post-office people and the grocer, so enforced these suggestions, that it was only when I was a boy of thirteen and fourteen . . . that . . . I began to question the final rightness of the gentlefolks, their primary necessity in the scheme of things. (I, i, 3)

Already, what one might call the "architectural rhetoric" of
Tono-Bungay begins to make itself felt. Reduced to logical terms,
what Wells is saying is that the great estates, like Bladesover,
were designed by people who enjoyed a privileged position in an
élitist society. But the concentration on the physical features of
the estate, rather than on the people who inhabit it (it is the
former which are particularized by epithets) attributes to these
physical features, themselves the creation of man, an unnatural
power over men; and this unnaturalness in the relationship
between men and their physical environment is one of Wells's
primary illustrations of the disorder in society as a whole. That
the architecture and layout of Bladesover can continue to
dominate the surrounding country long after the social order on
which it was built has become obsolete, eloquently represents the
failure of society to come to terms with the changes it has
experienced. The social fabric of England is undergoing a process
of change and decay, a process of which the inhabitants are
ironically and fatally unaware. The idea comes out in an
autumnal image:

> There are times when I wonder whether any but a very
> inconsiderable minority of English people realise how extensively
> this ostensible order has even now passed away. The great houses
> stand in the parks still, the cottages cluster respectfully on their
> borders, touching their eaves with their creepers . . .

(note the bold anthropomorphism here—the cottages stand in for
cottagers touching their forelocks)

> . . . the English countryside—you can range through Kent from
> Bladesover northward and see—persists obstinately in looking
> what it was. It is like an early day in a fine October. The hand of
> change rests on it all, unfelt, unseen; resting for awhile, as it were
> half reluctantly, before it grips and ends the thing for ever. One
> frost and the whole face of things will be bare, links snap, patience
> ends, our fine foliage of pretences lie glowing in the mire. (I, i, 3)

George recalls this image in the very last chapter of the novel:

> Other people may see this country in other terms; this is how I
> have seen it. In some early chapter in this heap I compared all
> our present colour and abundance to October foliage before the
> frosts nip down the leaves. That I still feel was a good image.
> Perhaps I see wrongly. It may be that I see decay all about me

because I am, in a sense, decay. To others it may be a scene of achievement and construction radiant with hope. I, too, have a sort of hope, but it is a remote hope, a hope that finds no promise in this Empire or in any of the great things of our time. (IV, iii, 1)

There may be an element of anarchic glee in the contemplation of this inevitable decay. But it is very far from being a revolutionary spirit. Misgiving, fear, even regret for lost beauty, are the dominant overtones in these images. We find in *Tono-Bungay* in fact, that submission of Wells's professed radical optimism to the more pessimistic intuitions of his imagination, which Bernard Bergonzi has located as a prime source of the enduring interest of Wells's science fiction.* Whereas Wells the scientific propagandist is associated in our minds with facile optimism and Progress-worship, *The Time Machine* is one of the most desolating myths in modern literature. And it is worth invoking at this point Robert Conquest's definition of science fiction as a distinct genre: "science fiction ranges over every type of story in which the centre of attention is on the results of a possible, though not actual, change in the conditions of life." [16] In *Tono-Bungay* Wells is concerned with the actual rather than with the possible (though he crosses the frontier in the quap episode). But the important point is that he is concerned with change in the "conditions of life"—a concern that, as Conquest points out, necessarily conflicts with the traditional concerns of the novel form, "the variations of human feelings and actions within contexts which are taken for granted." [17]

Though George recognizes that Bladesover is given over to change, the nature of the change invests the old obsolete Bladesover with a kind of virtue. George jumps forward in time, at the end of the first Book of the novel, to describe a visit, much later in his life, to Bladesover under the tenancy of Sir Reuben Lichtenstein. Bladesover under Lady Drew, he reflects, although obsolete and reactionary, had enshrined certain values. "About that park there were some elements of a liberal education . . .

---

* [Bernard Bergonzi, "*The Time Machine*: An Ironic Myth." It is included in this volume.—Ed.]

[16] Robert Conquest, "Science Fiction and Literature," *Critical Quarterly*, V (1963), p. 358.

[17] *Ibid.*, p. 356.

there was mystery, there was matter for the imagination" (I, i, 5). And the big saloon had housed books which, even if unread by their owners, helped a servant's son to a surreptitious education. Against the description of Lady Drew's saloon and its literary treasures is deliberately contrasted a description of the same room under the Lichtensteins:

> When I came back at last to the real Bladesover on an inconsequent visit, everything was far smaller than I could have supposed possible. It was as though everything had shivered and shrivelled a little at the Lichtenstein touch. The harp was still in the saloon, but there was a different grand piano with a painted lid and a metrostyle pianola, and an extraordinary quantity of artistic litter and *bric à brac* scattered about. There was the trail of the Bond Street showroom over it all. (I, ii, 8)

The detailed description continues for many lines. We are never at any point informed about the Lichtensteins as individuals. George passes directly from the account of their domestic furnishings to generalizations about their class. Bladesover is thus made into an *exemplum* of the decay of the social organism as a whole.

> The Lichtensteins and their like seem to have no promise in them at all of any fresh vitality for the kingdom. I do not believe in their intelligence or their power—they have nothing new about them at all, nothing creative or rejuvenescent, no more than a disorderly instinct of acquisition, and the prevalence of them and their kind is a phase in the broad slow decay of the great social organism of England. They could not have made Bladesover, they cannot replace it; they just happen to break out over it—saprophytically. (I, ii, 8)

The final, arresting metaphor (a saprophyte is "any vegetable organism which lives on decayed vegetable matter"—O.E.D.) makes vividly concrete the sustained image of England as an organism in which growth has become decay. On this note the first Book of *Tono-Bungay* ends.

The analysis of the condition of England in *Tono-Bungay* is dramatized throughout as a heuristic process in the narrator. As a child he did not question the fixed and stratified society represented by Lady Drew's Bladesover. "When I was a little boy

I took the place with the entirest faith as a complete authentic microcosm. I believed that the Bladesover system was a little working model—and not so very little either—of the whole world" (I, i, 3). Even when he is permitted to be a playmate of the Honourable Beatrice Normandy, the two children play with a microcosm of the microcosm, "the great doll's house that the Prince Regent had given Sir Harry Drew's first born (who died at five), that was a not ineffectual model of Bladesover itself, and contained eighty-five dolls and had cost hundreds of pounds" (I, i, 7). Although George quickly discovers that Lady Drew's Bladesover is not a microcosm of the modern world, its importance as a clue to the social anatomy of England is not diminished:

> . . . in a sense Bladesover has never left me; it is, as I said at the outset, one of those dominant explanatory impressions that make the framework of my mind. Bladesover illuminates England; it has become all that is spacious, dignified, pretentious, and truly conservative in English life. It is my social datum. That is why I have drawn it here on so large a scale. (I, ii, 8)

George's first realization that there is an uglier, more sinister aspect of English life than that represented by Bladesover, comes when he is exiled to Chatham, after he has disgraced himself by fighting Beatrice's half-brother Archie. This realization is partly formed by George's misery in the mean, dismal life of his chapel-going cousins, the Frapps (one of whom, George says, "I am now convinced, had some secret disease that drained his vitality away" (I, i, 1)); but the dominant impression is of Chatham, and its neighbour Rochester, as *places*, as the antithesis of Bladesover. The large, free, assured handling of townscape in this section, while at the same time sustaining a polemical argument, is characteristic of *Tono-Bungay*. But Wells reserves his most powerful effects in this mode for London.

In Kent, the great estates have managed to keep the ugliness and squalor of industry at a distance; but in London, as George sees, once more in architectural terms, the two forces are engaged at close quarters. As a young student, George explores the city, and out of this exploration, he says, "there has grown up in me a kind of theory of London" (II, i. I). It is a theory that again takes Bladesover as its starting point, and is again darkened by allusion to disease:

. . . I do think I see lines of an ordered structure out of which it [London] has grown, detected a process that is something more than a confusion of casual accidents, though indeed it may be no more than a process of disease.

I said at the outset of my first book that I find in Bladesover the clue to all England. Well, I certainly imagine it is the clue to the structure of London. There have been no revolutions, no deliberate restatements or abandonments of opinion in England since the days of the fine gentry; since 1688 or thereabouts, the days when Bladesover was built; there have been changes, dissolving forces, replacing forces if you will; but then it was that the broad lines of the English system set firmly. And as I have gone to and fro in London, in certain regions the thought has recurred, this is Bladesover House, this answers to Bladesover House. The fine gentry may have gone; they have indeed largely gone, I think; rich merchants may have replaced them, financial adventurers or what not. That does not matter; the shape is still Bladesover. (II, i, 1)

He then traces out what he regards as the "Great-House region" of London, the residential areas around the West End Parks. It is an enlargement of Bladesover—the National History museum corresponding to the cases of stuffed birds on the Bladesover staircase, the Art Museum to the Bladesover curios and porcelain, and so on.

It is this idea of escaping parts from the seventeenth-century system of Bladesover, of proliferating and overgrowing elements from the Estates, that to this day seems to me the best explanation, not simply of London, but of all England. England is a country of great Renaissance landed gentlefolk who have been unconsciously outgrown and overgrown. (II, i, 1)

The landed gentlefolk have been outgrown and overgrown by the new rich, who have preserved, if vulgarized, the architectural fabric they have parasitically occupied. ("In the meanwhile the old shapes, the old attitudes remain, subtly changed and changing still, sheltering strange tenants" (I, i, 3).) But both orders are threatened "by the presence of great new forces, blind forces of invasion, of growth."

The railway termini on the north side of London have been kept as remote as Eastry had kept the railway station from Wimblehurst, they stop on the very outskirts of the estates, but from the south, the South Eastern railway had butted its great stupid rusty iron head of Charing Cross station—that great head that came smashing down in 1905—clean across the river, between Somerset House and Whitehall. The south side had no protecting estates. Factory chimneys smoke right over against Westminster with an air of carelessly not having permission, and the whole effect of industrial London and of all London east of Temple Bar and of the huge dingy immensity of London port, is to me of something disproportionately large, something morbidly expanded, without plan or intention, dark and sinister toward the clean clear social assurance of the West End. And south of this central London, south-east, south-west, far west, north-west, all round the northern hills, are similar disproportionate growths, endless streets of undistinguished houses, undistinguished industries, shabby families, second-rate shops, inexplicable people who in a once fashionable phrase, do no 'exist'. All these aspects have suggested to my mind at times, do suggest to this day, the unorganized, abundant substance of some tumourous growth-process, a process which indeed bursts all the outlines of the affected carcass and protrudes such masses as ignoble comfortable Croydon, as tragic impoverished West Ham. To this day I ask myself will those masses ever become structural, will they indeed shape into anything new whatever, or is that cancerous image their true and ultimate diagnosis . . . ? (II, i, 1)

Speaking as a Londoner, I can think of few writers who have succeeded as well in constructing a comprehensive image of the metropolis as Wells in this passage. The passing of time has affected its validity to a very small extent. There are still tragic and impoverished areas of London, still comfortable and ignoble areas. The endless streets of undistinguished houses still depress the eye and bewilder the mind. Above all, the architectural contrasts around the banks of the Thames, which Wells renders so vividly, still seem to embody the confusion and conflict of values in the capital, and in society as a whole.

The movement of the passage illustrates very well how in *Tono-Bungay* Wells's analytic, Fabian radicalism is transposed into a literary and imaginative key. Beginning with a *datum* of social history (the locations of the London railway termini) we are swiftly introduced to a vision of boldly anthropomorphized architecture and engineering (the Charing Cross railway station, the South Bank chimneys) in which these material objects seem to be more alive than the people that use them. The parallel with Dickens's Coketown is striking. But Wells exploits the unnaturalness of the contrast more deliberately, in order to reintroduce his thematic image of decay. Wells, as one would expect, chooses his pathological metaphors with care. Cancer is the perfect metaphorical diagnosis of the condition of England, for cancer has an organic life of its own, which is however unnatural and malignant. It is also a disease which often goes long undetected by those who suffer from it. To quote the *O.E.D.* again, cancer is "a malignant growth or tumour, that tends to reproduce itself; it corrodes the part concerned, and generally ends in death." This image thus draws together the two predominant strains in the language of descriptive comment in the novel: words suggestive of growth, change, and movement; and words suggestive of decay and death.

On the narrative level, the principal vehicle of Wells's critique of modern capitalism is the story of Edward Ponderevo's rise and fall. Wells demonstrates wittily and persuasively how bold and unscrupulous methods of sales-promotion applied to a worthless and indeed mildly injurious product can obtain for a man of no real ability, immense power, wealth, and prestige. Kettle complains that Wells does not condemn Ponderevo with adequate severity.[18] But it is surely Wells's point that Ponderevo is a foolish, childishly innocent man, that it is society, which puts this colossal power into his hands, which is ultimately responsible. "This irrational muddle of a community in which we live gave him that [his wealth], paid him at that rate for sitting in a room and scheming and telling it lies" (III, i, 2). George does not attempt to soften his contempt for Ponderevo's enterprises and his own part in them:

> he created nothing, he invented nothing, he economised nothing. I cannot claim that a single one of the great businesses we organised added any real value to human life at all.

The "frame" of architectural and topographical description "gets into the picture" of Ponderevo's career in a very significant way. When for example, in the early days of "Tono-Bungay,"

[18] Kettle, *op. cit.*, p. 98.

George is hesitating between his uncle's offer of a partnership and the arduous and demanding career of a scientist, he goes for a solitary walk in London to meditate:

> And as I walked along the Embankment, the first effect was all against my uncle. He shrank—for a little while he continued to shrink—in perspective until he was only a very small shabby little man in a dirty back street, selling off a few hundred bottles of rubbish to foolish buyers. The great buildings on the right of us, the Inns and the School Board place—as it was then—Somerset House, the big hotels, the great bridges, Westminster's outlines ahead, had an effect of grey largeness that reduced him to the proportions of a busy black beetle in a crack in the floor.
>
> And then my eye caught the advertisements on the south side of "Sorber's Food," of "Cracknell's Ferric Wine," very bright and prosperous signs, illuminated at night, and I realised how astonishingly they looked at home there, how evidently they were part of the whole thing. (II, ii, 3)

This passage draws for its effect upon the more elaborate description of London quoted above: in both, the new world of vulgar commerce jauntily confronts the old order across the Thames. And as George walks on, he realizes that a bridgehead has been established across which the new forces are already swarming. Again and again, on hoardings in Adelphi terrace and Kensington High Street, the strident advertisements for "Tono-Bungay" catch his eye. With a helpless shrug, he dismisses his dreams of the good society and joins his uncle.

Each stage in Ponderevo's rapid rise to fame and wealth is marked by an account of his changing domestic environment, conducted in such a way as to provide an ironic comment upon the absurdity of Ponderevo's career. That Ponderevo should use his newly acquired wealth to improve his domestic environment is natural. But his constant moving from house to house (described mainly in the long second chapter of Book III, "Our Progress from Camden Town to Crest Hill") is motivated less and less by considerations of comfort, convenience, and suitability, and more and more by a desire to emulate Bladesover. This desire is only partly conscious in Ponderevo, and is to some extent resisted by his more sensible and sympathetic wife; but it is inescapable and insatiable, an infection of the utter confusion of values in which they live.

As soon as the first money from *Tono-Bungay* begins to roll in, the Ponderevos move to a flat in Gower Street. George notes on his first visit: "the furniture of the room struck upon my eye as almost stately. The chairs and sofa were covered with chintz, which gave it a dim remote flavour of Bladesover" (II, ii, 6). Soon Ponderevo buys a villa in Beckenham, "with a conservatory and a shrubbery, a tennis-lawn, a quite considerable vegetable garden, and a small disused coach-house" (III, ii, 1). No sooner, however, has Susan Ponderevo begun to settle happily in Beckenham society, than she is uprooted to Chislehurst.

> The Chislehurst mansion had "grounds" rather than a mere garden, and there was a gardener's cottage and a little lodge at the gate. (III, ii, 3)

But no imitation of Bladesover can satisfy Ponderevo. In Lady Grove he acquires a Bladesover of his own. George's leisurely, appreciative description recalls his account of Bladesover:

> Lady Grove, you know, is a very beautiful house indeed, a still and gracious place, whose age-long seclusion was only effectively broken with the toot of the coming of the motor-car. . . . An old Catholic family had died out in it, century by century, and was now altogether dead. . . . Its terrace is its noblest feature, a very wide broad lawn it is, bordered by a low stone battlement, and there is a great cedar in one corner under whose level branches one looks out across the blue distances of the Weald—blue distances that are made extraordinarily Italian in quality by virtue of the dark masses of that single tree. . . . One turns back to the still old house, and sees a gray and lichenous façade with a very finely arched entrance. It was warmed by the afternoon light and touched with the colour of a few neglected roses and pyrancanthus. . . . And there was my uncle holding his goggles in a sealskin glove, wiping the glass with a pocket-handkerchief, and asking my aunt if Lady Grove wasn't a "Bit of all Right." My aunt made him no answer. (III, ii, 6)

"Numbers go down in the competition," says Masterman, in *The Condition of England*, "then the country estates are sold and pass into the hands of South African millionaires or the children of the big traders, or the vendors of patent medicines." [19]

Ill at ease among the ghosts of Lady Grove, Ponderevo will not

---

[19] Masterman, *op. cit.*, p. 35.

rest until he has not only emulated but exceeded Bladesover, until he has built himself a new Bladesover, "a Twentieth Century house" (III, ii, 10): Crest Hill. Crest Hill marks the climax of Ponderevo's career, epitome of his inflated wealth, his irresponsibility and his delusions of grandeur:

> There he stands in my memory, the symbol of this age for me, the man of luck and advertisement, the current master of the world. There he stands upon the great outward sweep of the terrace before the huge main entrance, a little figure, ridiculously disproportionate to that forty-foot arch, with the granite ball behind him—the astronomical ball, brass coopered, that represented the world. . . . There he stands, Napoleonically grouped with his retinue . . . below are hundreds of feet of wheeling planks, ditches, excavations, heaps of earth, piles of garden-stone from the Wealden ridges. On either hand the walls of his irrelevant unmeaning palace rise. At one time he had working in that place—disturbing the economic balance of the whole countryside by their presence—upwards of three thousand men. . . .
>
> So he poses for my picture amidst the raw beginnings that were never to be completed. He did the strangest things about that place, things more and more detached from any conception of financial scale, things more and more apart from sober humanity. He seemed to think himself at last quite released from any such limitations. He moved quite a considerable hill, and nearly sixty mature trees were moved with it to open his prospect eastward, moved it about two hundred feet to the south. At another time he caught a suggestion from some city restaurant and made a billiard-room roofed with plate glass beneath the waters of his ornamental lake. He furnished one wing while its roof still awaited completion. He had a swimming bath thirty feet square next to his bedroom upstairs, and to crown it all he commenced a great wall to hold all his dominions together, free from the invasion of common man. It was a ten-foot wall, glass-surmounted, and had it been completed as he intended it, it would have had a total length of nearly eleven miles. Some of it towards the last was so dishonestly built that it collapsed within a year upon its foundations, but some miles of it still stand. I never think of it now but what I think of the hundreds of eager little investors who followed his "star," whose hopes and lives, whose wives' security and children's prospects are all mixed up beyond redemption with that flaking mortar. (III, ii, 10)

Wells needs to be quoted at length, for his effects are broad and cumulative. He did not, like James, pursue "the grace of intensity." But the language of this passage has its own kind of expressive effectiveness. The rather loose, conversational syntax of the second paragraph, its rather clumsy repetitions (*moved* in the fourth sentence, *it* in the eighth and ninth), and its abundance of figures and measurements, establish the tone of a man who is striving to make a fantastic event credible, to compel our assent to this particular event.* But the mock portentous repetition of "there he stands . . ." supports the invitation to see Ponderevo as a symbolic figure, symbolic not only of commercial vulgarity but of commercial megalomania. While Ponderevo's previous vanities had been merely comic, his activities at Crest Hill have a lunatic unnatural quality, "a quality," as George puts it, "of unforseeing outrage upon the peace of nature" (III, ii, 10) which is implied in Ponderevo's re-shaping of the landscape. The disturbance of nature echoes the disturbance of the economic balance; the dishonestly-built walls reflect Ponderevo's dishonestly-earned fortune; and their collapse foreshadows his financial collapse. Characteristically, the emblematic description becomes fully metaphorical in the next paragraph:

> It is curious how many of these modern financiers of chance and bluff have ended their careers by building. It was not merely my uncle. Sooner or later they all seem to bring their luck to the test of realisation, try to make their fluid opulence coagulate out as bricks and mortar, bring moonshine into relations with a weekly-wages sheet. Then the whole fabric of confidence and imagination totters—and down they come. . . . (III, ii, 10)

Wells brilliantly rounds off the architectural commentary upon Ponderevo's career in the scene of his death, in which irony and pathos are so skilfully mingled. In his last delirium Ponderevo raves of a still more grandiose building, a financier's new Jerusalem:

* Masterman describes an "England where millionaire company promoters, on their hectic path between poverty through prosperity to prison or suicide [*sic*], will purchase so many miles of good English land, build round it a great wall ten feet high, construct billiard rooms under a lake, move a hill that offends the view" (*op. cit.*, p. 28). Masterman is obviously describing Crest Hill here, but he offers the description as one from real life. Whether Masterman was conscious or unconscious of his source at this point, he testifies to Wells's success in making Crest Hill a convincing and representative enterprise.

> "What is this great place, these cloud-capped towers, these airy
> pinnacles? . . . Ilion. Sky-y-pointing . . . Ilion House, the res-
> idence of one of our great merchant princes . . . Terrace above
> terrace. Reaching to the Heavens . . . Kingdoms Caesar never
> knew. . . . A great poet, George. Zzzz. Kingdoms Caesar never
> knew. . . . Under entirely new management. (IV, i, 7)

This recalls another visionary city in *Tono-Bungay*: the City of
Women envisaged by Ewart, George's bohemian, idealistic,
revolutionary friend as an answer to the sexual problems of the
age:

> "I seem to see—I seem to see—a sort of City of Women,
> Ponderevo. Yes . . . a walled enclosure—good stone-mason's
> work—a city wall, high as the walls of Rome, going about a
> garden. Dozens of square miles of garden—trees—fountains—
> arbours—lakes. Lawns on which the women play, avenues in
> which they gossip, boats. . . . And no man—except to do rough
> work perhaps,—ever comes in. . . . The homes of the women,
> Ponderevo, will be set in the walls of their city. . . . Built into the
> wall—and a little balcony. . . . And men will stroll up and down
> there when they feel the need of feminine company. . . . And
> each woman will have this; she will have a little silken ladder she
> can let down if she chooses—if she wants to talk closer. . . ." (II,
> iv, 3)

Thus the architectural "frame" gets into the picture of the sexual
relationships of the novel. That George's marriage to Marion is
doomed is conveyed from the start by the home in which he finds
her, and the house and furnishings Marion insists upon when
they are married. "All our conceptions of life differed. I
remember how we differed about furniture" (II, iv, 5). The
wedding itself is put in the larger perspective of the condition of
England.

> Under the stress of tradition we were all of us trying in the
> fermenting chaos of London to carry out the marriage ceremonies
> of a Bladesover tenant or one of the chubby middling sort of
> people in some dependent country town. (II, iv, 4)

So far, we have seen how Wells depicts England in topographical
and architectural terms as an organism undergoing a process of
change. For him, as for Masterman, "arises the question of the
future of a society, evidently moving in a direction which no one

can forsee, towards experience of far-reaching change." [20] As radicals, both men saw the necessity of change, but the change they saw in progress was not of a rational or fruitful kind. Wells saw it as a process of disease and decay. "Again and again in this book," says George at the end of *Tono-Bungay*, "I have written of England as a feudal scheme overtaken by fatty degeneration and stupendous accidents of hypertrophy" (IV, iii, 2).* It is this governing idea of change as disease and decay which, I think, connects the "quap" episode to the total design of *Tono-Bungay*, and provides an answer to those critics who have seen it as an irrelevant intrusion.†

In his *Anatomy of Criticism*, Northrop Frye makes the following reference to *Tono-Bungay*:

> The destroyer which appears at the end of H. G. Wells's *Tono-Bungay* is notable as coming from a low mimetic writer not much given to introducing hieratic symbols. [21]

A certain amount of elucidation of Frye's terminology may be advisable. He divides the literary modes into five classes: mythic, romantic, high mimetic (epic and tragedy), low mimetic (comedy and realistic fiction), and ironic. He regards this system as a cycle corresponding to the historical development of literature, according to which modern literature is dominated by the low

---

[20] *Ibid.,* p. 18.

* Cf. the deterioration of Ponderevo's physique as his wealth and power increase. George notices how, compared to his appearance at Wimblehurst, his head seems to have shrunk and his belly expanded, though "he evidently wasn't aware of the *degenerative* nature of his changes" *(my italics)* (II, ii, 2). George himself becomes ashamed of "the slackness of body and soul that had come to me with the business life" (III, iii, 1) and goes into rigorous training.

† E.g. "It is brilliantly done, but it is plainly an afterthought" (Walter Allen, *The English Novel*, p. 317). "Wells, for all his energy, often flags towards the end of a book—not, I feel sure, because his imagination was exhausted, but merely because he wanted to get on with something else and was impatient with the work in hand. Towards the end of *Tono-Bungay* he had this desire for a change, but satisfied it by incorporating the new material in the same book" (Norman Nicholson, *H. G. Wells* (1950), p. 65. No external evidence is cited). The only critic who, to my knowledge, has recognized the thematic connection between the "quap" episode and the rest of the novel, is Gordon N. Ray, "H. G. Wells Tries to Be a Novelist," *Edwardians and Late Victorians*, English Institute Essays, 1959, edited by Richard Ellmann (New York, 1960), p. 147.

[21] Northrop Frye, *Anatomy of Criticism: Four essays* (Princeton, 1957), p. 155.

mimetic and ironic modes. Since the system *is* a cycle, however, the ironic mode tends to return to the mythic—Joyce being the most obvious example.[22] Frye characterizes Wells as a low mimetic writer, whose mode is defined thus:

> If superior neither to other men nor to his environment, the hero is one of us: We respond to a sense of his common humanity, and demand from the poet the same canons of probability that we find in our own experience. This gives us the hero of the *low mimetic* mode, of most comedy and realistic fiction.[23]

If we take England, rather than George Ponderevo, to be the hero of *Tono-Bungay*, however, that novel fits very neatly into Frye's definition of the ironic mode:

> If inferior in power or intelligence to ourselves, so that we have the sense of looking down on a scene of bondage, frustration, or absurdity, the hero belongs to the ironic mode. This is still true when the reader feels that he is or might be in the same situation, as the situation is being judged by the norms of a greater freedom.[24]

Given Frye's notion of the contiguity of the ironic and the mythic modes on the literary-historical cycle, it now seems more likely that Wells should resort to hieratic symbols—that is, symbols whose meanings have accreted in the mythical, romantic and high mimetic modes. Frye himself remarks that science fiction is "a mode of romance with a strong inherent tendency to myth";[25] and Bernard Bergonzi, using Frye's conceptual framework, has made a fascinating analysis of demonic and paradisal symbolism in *The Time Machine*.[26] I suggest that the "quap" in *Tono-Bungay* is another example of this dimension in Wells's writing.

The quap is first described to George and his uncle by an adventurer, Gordon-Naysmith, who discovered it on the coast of West Africa, as

> the most radio-active stuff in the world. That's quap! It's a festering mass of earths and heavy metals, polonium, radium,

[22] *Ibid.*, p. 42.
[23] *Ibid.*, p. 34.
[24] *Ibid.*, p. 34.
[25] *Ibid.*, p. 49.
[26] Bernard Bergonzi, *The Early H. G. Wells, A Study of the Scientific Romances* (Manchester, 1961), pp. 52–3. ["*The Time Machine*: An Ironic Myth" from this is included earlier in this volume.—Ed.]

ythorium, carium, and new things too. There's a stuff called Xk—provisionally. There they are all mucked up together in sort of rotting sand. What it is, how it got made, I don't know. It's like as if some young creator had been playing about there. There it lies in two heaps, one small, one great, and the world for miles about it is blasted and scorched and dead. (III, i, 4)

The concept of a morbid kind of life, spreading decay and death, is immediately established, and is confirmed by George's subsequent paraphrase: "he gave a sense of heat and a perpetual reek of vegetable decay . . . among charred dead weeds stands the abandoned station—abandoned because every man who stayed two months in that station stayed to die, eaten up mysteriously like a leper—with its dismantled sheds and its decaying pier of worm-rotten and oblique piles and planks . . ." (III, i, 4).

Not until Ponderevo is faced with bankruptcy, and the development of a new type of filament has made the mineral content of the quap fantastically valuable, does George decide to take a ship to Africa and (illegally) confiscate the quap. The expedition is cursed with ill luck from the beginning. George and his men get sick. Finally, the quap, which has been obtained at such great cost, rots the hull of the ship in which it is carried back to England, and it sinks. The last desperate attempt to rescue the declining fortunes of Ponderevo has failed.

Seen as an action, the episode has obvious analogies with the archetypal story of the quest for a treasure which brings death to the questors, of which Chaucer's *Pardoner's Tale* is a well-known example. Particularly interesting in this respect is the psychological effect of the expedition on George and his crew. It makes them sullen, ill-tempered, and quarrelsome, and finally impels George to the motiveless murder of an African native (III, iv, 6).

But throughout the quap episode, physical deterioration is emphasized as much as moral deterioration. George and the crew "were poisoned, I firmly believe, by quap" (III, iv, 3). Sores break out on the crew's hands when they handle the quap (III, iv, 5). At night there hangs over the quap-heaps "a phosphorescence such as one sees at times on rotting wood" (III, iv, 3). This insistence upon disease and decay echoes at several points the metaphorical language in which Wells describes the disintegration of the English social organism. The connection is made explicit in the following passage:

If I am right it is something far more significant from the scientific point of view than those incidental constituents of various rare metals, pitchblende, rutile, and the like, upon which the revolutionary discoveries of the last decade are based. Those are just little molecular centres of disintegration, of that mysterious decay and rotting of those elements, elements once regarded as the most stable things in nature. But there is something—the only word that comes near it is *cancerous*—and that is not very near, about the whole of quap, something that creeps and lives as a disease lives by destroying; an elemental stirring and disarrangement, incalculably maleficent and strange.

This is no imaginative comparison of mine. To my mind radioactivity is a real disease of matter. Moreover, it is a contagious disease. It spreads. You bring these debased and crumbling atoms near others and those too presently catch the trick of swinging themselves out of coherent existence. *It is in matter exactly what the decay of our old culture is in society, a loss of traditions and distinctions and assured reactions (my italics).* When I think of these inexplicable dissolvent centres that have come into being in our globe . . . I am haunted by a grotesque fancy of the ultimate eating away and dry-rotting and dispersal of all our world. So that while man still struggles and dreams his very substance will change and crumble from beneath him. I mention this here as a queer persistent fancy. Suppose that is, indeed, to be the end of our planet; no splendid climax and finale, no towering accumulation of achievements but just—atomic decay! I add that to the ideas of the suffocating comet, the dark body out of space, the burning out of the sun, the distorted orbit, as a new and far more possible end—as Science can see ends to this strange by-play of matter that we call human life. (III, iv, 5)

This is another passage whose thematic importance is conveyed by its verbal excitement, and, like other such passages in *Tono-Bungay*, it is not much concerned with individual character and action. It is clotted with words connotative or denotative of disease and decay: *disease* (3), *decay* (3), *disintegration, disarrangement, rotting, dry-rotting, cancerous, contagious, destroying, debased, maleficent, crumble, crumbling, dissolvent, eating away, dispersal.* This profusion is not, however, tautological. The elaborate description of the quap strikes echoes at various points with other parts of the descriptive "frame" of the novel. *Disease, contagious,* and the italicized *cancerous* link up with other pathological metaphors in the novel, particularly in the description of London. *Dry-rotting, crumble, crumbling, eating away,* and *disintegration* are terms which might be applied to material structures, such as buildings. One recalls George's description of England as "this rotten old warren" (III, iii, 7). In this passage, as throughout the novel, *change* is associated with *decay.*

The immediate justification for the plethora of epithets is that the narrator is struggling to give definition to a half-apprehended *something:* "There is *something* . . . cancerous . . . *something* that creeps and lives as a disease. . . ." Throughout the novel George speaks in the same tone of a man trying urgently to define something new, unrecognized, threatening. Compare the passage on London again: "The effect . . . is to me of *something* disproportionately large, *something* morbidly expanded. . . ."

These verbal interrelationships with the total fabric of the novel enforce and confirm the explicit connection George makes between the quap and the condition of England. It is difficult therefore to sustain the charge that the episode is an irrelevance. Seeking wealth to revive the failing Ponderevo fortune, George discovers an enormously valuable but death-dealing treasure. Coming from a decadent and disintegrating "civilized" society he encounters in the primitive jungle a frightening tangible agent of decay and disintegration. And in words which remind us irresistibly of the pessimistic myths of Wells's science fiction, the threat of the quap is expanded to embrace the destiny of the entire race.

For all its vividness and power, the quap symbol is not allowed to dominate *Tono-Bungay.* The frame of architectural and topographical description remains the principal vehicle for the themes of the novel. It is the only constant element in a novel which is otherwise deliberately chaotic in structure, and it fittingly dominates the very last chapter: "Night and the Open Sea," in which George describes a cruise down the Thames in the X_2, a destroyer he has designed.

> It is curious how at times one's impressions will all fuse and run together into a sort of unity and become continuous with things that have hitherto been utterly alien and remote. That rush down the river became mysteriously connected with this book. As I passed down the Thames I seemed in a new and parallel manner to be passing all England in review. I saw it then as I had wanted my readers to see it. (IV, iii, 2)

The pages which follow need to be read continuously; I can only extract a few passages in which the motifs of the novel are most conspicuously recalled.

Wells sees the Thames as cutting an historical cross-section through England, in which the past is fossilized in the scenery and architecture of the banks.

> One begins in Craven Reach and it is as if one were in the heart of old England. Behind us are Kew and Hampton Court with their memories of Kings and Cardinals and one runs at first between Fulham's episcopal garden parties and Hurlingham's playground for the sporting instinct of our race. The whole effect is English. There is space, there are old trees and all the best qualities of the homeland in that upper reach. Putney, too, looks Anglican on a dwindling scale. And then for a stretch the newer developments slop over, one misses Bladesover and there come first squalid stretches of mean homes right and left and then the dingy industrialism of the south side, and on the north bank the polite long front of nice houses, artistic, literary, administrative people's residences, that stretches from Cheyne Walk nearly to Westminster and hides a wilderness of slums. (IV, ii, 2)

Once more the symbolic confrontation of north and south banks is introduced, the north bank feebly keeping up the old pretence, the south bank unashamed of its modern barbarism. After St. Paul's:

> the traditional and ostensible England falls from you altogether . . . the trim scheme of the old order is altogether dwarfed and swallowed up. . . . Again and again in this book I have written of England as a feudal scheme overtaken by fatty degeneration and stupendous accidents of hypertrophy. For the last time I must strike that note as the memory of the dear, neat little sunlit ancient Tower of London lying away in a gap among the warehouses comes back to me, that little accumulation of buildings so provincially pleasant and dignified, overshadowed by the vulgarest, most typical exploit of modern England, the sham Gothic casings to the ironwork of the Tower Bridge. That Tower Bridge is the very balance and confirmation of Westminster's dull pinnacles and tower. That sham Gothic bridge; in the very gates of our mother of change, the Sea! (IV, iii, 2)

No passage could better illustrate Wells's literary strategy in *Tono-Bungay*: to present England as an organism undergoing a process of change and decay, both the organism and the process being depicted in terms of architectural and topographical description. The irony of the situation is that England is unaware of its condition, or ignores it. In the Houses of Parliament a debased oligarchy goes through the motions of its "incurable tradition of commercialized Bladesovery" (note the pathological epithet), its futile attempts to pretend that nothing has changed being aptly symbolized by another pseudo-Gothic building, Tower Bridge, placed "in the very gates of our mother of change."

> For the third part of the panorama of London is beyond all law, order, and precedence, it is the seaport and the sea. One goes down the widening reaches through a monstrous variety of shipping, great steamers, great sailing-ships, trailing the flags of all the world, a monstrous confusion of lighters, witches' confer- ence of brown-sailed barges, wallowing tugs, a tumultuous crowding and jostling of cranes and spars, and wharves and stores, and assertive inscriptions. Huge vistas of dock open right and left of one, and here and there beyond and amidst it all are church towers, little patches of indescribably old-fashioned and worn-out houses, riverside pubs and the like, vestiges of townships that were long since torn to fragments and submerged in these new growths. And amidst it all no plan appears, no intention, no comprehen- sive desire. That is the very key of it all. Each day one feels that the pressure of commerce grew, grew insensibly monstrous, and first this man made a wharf and then that, and so they jostled together to make this unassimilable enormity of traffic. Through it we dodged and drove, eager for the high seas. (IV, ii, 2)

This is a brilliantly vivid description, the congestion of diction and syntax imitating the congestion of the scene. But again one observes the consistency of the tone with other heightened descriptions in the novel. The twice-repeated *monstrous* evokes the same kind of fear as the image of London as a huge corpse swollen with cancer, or as the account of the sinister properties of quap. There is the same insistence on the lack of *plan* or *intention* as in the earlier description of London. There is the familiar association of growth with destruction ("torn to fragments or submerged in these new growths"). There is the familiar trick of attributing life to things rather than to people. There is the characteristic search for a *key* to the spectacle of anarchy.

Why is George so eager for the high seas? It is evidently not because of a desire to escape from Change, since the sea is the Mother of change. Rather it is a gesture of acceptance of change. George rushes to embrace the destructive element, figuring in his voyage the inevitable decline and extinction of his country, and finding a kind of freedom in this pessimistic vision:

> Out to the open [sea] we go, to windy freedom and trackless ways. Light after light goes down. England and the Kingdom, Britain and the Empire, the old prides and the old devotions, glide abeam, astern, sink down upon the horizon, pass—pass. The river passes, England passes . . . (IV, iii, 2)

It is a mood akin to that of *The Waste Land.*

> What is the city over the mountains
> Cracks and reforms and bursts in the violet air
> Falling towers
> Jerusalem Athens Alexandria
> Vienna London
> Unreal [27]

Whereas the pessimism of Eliot's poem is qualified by the counsels of oriental mysticism, the pessimism of *Tono-Bungay* is qualified by what might be described as scientific mysticism: "The note that sounds clear in my mind when I think of anything beyond the purely personal aspects of my story," says George, invoking for the last time the key-words of his descriptive frame, "is a note of crumbling and confusion, of change and seemingly aimless swelling, of a bubbling up and medley of futile loves and sorrows."

> But through the confusion sounds another note. Through the confusion something drives, something that is at once human achievement and the most inhuman of all existing things. . . . I have figured it in my last section by the symbol of my destroyer, stark and swift, irrelevant to most human interests. Sometimes I call this reality Science, sometimes I call it Truth. But it is something we draw by pain and effort out of the heart of life, that we disentangle and make clear. (IV, iii, 3)

The striking of this final note has been much criticized. Mark Schorer, for instance, has this to say:

[27] "The Waste Land" ll. 371–6.

The significant failure is in that end, and in the way that it defeats not only the entire social analysis of the bulk of the novel, but Wells's own ends as a thinker. For at last George finds a purpose in science. "I decided that in power and knowledge lay the salvation of my life, the secret that would fill my need; that to these things I would give myself."

But science, power and knowledge, are summed up at last in a destroyer. As far as one can tell Wells intends no irony, although he may here have come upon the essence of the major irony in modern history. The novel ends in a kind of meditative rhapsody which denies every value that the book has been aiming toward. For of all the kinds of social waste which Wells has been describing, this is the most inclusive, the final waste.[28]

But is it true that Wells intends no irony? Certainly, in so far as the destroyer is an achievement of engineering, it represents a kind of scientific equivalent of that impersonal fulfilment and unity of being which romantic and post-romantic poets have embodied in images of organic life or of perfectly achieved art. But Wells is fully aware of the irony of making this achievement a destroyer. "It is all one spectacle of forces running to waste," says George, recapitulating his story, "of people who use and do not replace, the story of a country hectic with a wasting aimless fever of trade and money-making and pleasure-seeking. And now I build destroyers!" (IV, iii, 1). The very name of the destroyer, "X2," recalls the name of the unidentified ingredient in quap, "Xk." By choosing a destroyer as his symbol, Wells indicates that in a social order given over to decay and death, even the impersonal achievements of science will be ironically double-edged; that they will hasten and confirm, rather than alleviate, the incurable condition of England. How then, does the intro-duction of the destroyer defeat Wells's social analysis in *Tono-Bungay*, which has been all along ironic and pessimistic? As to Wells's "ends as a thinker," *Tono-Bungay* is not the only one of his imaginative works which disturbingly questions the meliorism of his public self.

[28] Schorer, *op. cit.*, p. 73.

Tono-Bungay:
Tradition and Experiment

by Lucille Herbert

H. G. Wells's *Tono-Bungay* (1909) has long been regarded, in the author's own phrase, as his "finest and most finished novel upon the accepted lines." [1] Even before the first installment appeared in the *English Review*, Ford Madox Ford, who had happily accepted the novel for serial publication, told Wells that it had "all the qualities of the traditional classical English novel." [2] This view has prevailed ever since, though critics have disagreed about the precise character of the traditions supposed to operate in *Tono-Bungay* as well as about its literary merit. It has, for example, been variously described as "spiritual biography," [3] as a "Condition of England novel" in the manner of *Hard Times*,[4] and, by Wells himself, indiscriminately as a novel "on Dickens-Thackeray lines" and "a social panorama in the vein of Balzac." [5] Its place in literary history, however, remains the one that the author and his editor implicitly assigned to it. According to Wells's most distinguished recent critics, Bernard Bergonzi and Gordon N. Ray, *Tono-Bungay* marks the end of a novelistic tradition. It is "one of the last examples . . . of the panoramic

[1] Preface to *Tono-Bungay*, in *Works of H. G. Wells*, Atlantic Edition, XII (New York, 1925).

[2] *Letters of Ford Madox Ford*, ed. Richard M. Ludwig (Princeton, 1965), p. 29.

[3] Richard H. Costa, *H. G. Wells* (New York, 1967), p. 82.

[4] David Lodge, "*Tono-Bungay* and the Condition of England," *Language of Fiction* (New York, 1966), pp. 214–42. [Included in this volume as the preceding essay—Ed.]

[5] *Experiment in Autobiography* (New York, 1934), pp. 546, 423.

novel, of a kind familiar to the Victorians," [6] and Wells was "the last English novelist to write from a sense of society as a whole." [7]

Such unanimity among authorities would seem to be conclusive. Nevertheless, I should like to call for a general reconsideration of the narrative mode of *Tono-Bungay* and its significance for the history of English fiction. Mark Schorer has tellingly observed: "The novelist flounders through a series of literary imitations—from an early Dickensian episode, through a kind of Shavian interlude, through a Conradian episode, to a Jules Verne vision at the end." [8] Rather than assume, however, that Wells was merely trying to say what had been said before in the various narrative languages he borrowed and that he was unable to reconcile their discordant messages, it seems to me necessary to examine closely the attitudes that actually operate in his novel. If, as I believe I can show, there is a fundamental dissonance between the values, the interests, the conceptions of self and society that inform *Tono-Bungay* and those of the nineteenth-century authors whom Wells might be thought of as impersonating through the voice of his narrator, then some questions about the whole expressive method of the novel also demand attention. What are the functions and interrelationships of the imitated styles and traditional narrative patterns, and was Wells not, after all, seeking to contain these elements within a formal structure appropriate to his own view of human life and to the spirit of his own age as he conceived it? These questions really embrace a more specific one that lies behind the assertion that in the context of Wells's "panoramic" vision of a decaying society "the inert mass of George's 'private' story remains an unassimilated element in the novel." [9] What is the relation between the confessional or autobiographical form and content of *Tono-Bungay* and the intention Wells announced in his preface to the Atlantic Edition (1925) of giving "a view of the contemporary social and political system in Great Britain, an old and degenerating system . . ."?

[6] Bernard Bergonzi, introduction to *Tono-Bungay*, Riverside Edition (Boston, 1966), p. xxiii. All quotations from *Tono-Bungay* are from this edition.

[7] Gordon N. Ray, "H. G. Wells Tries to Be a Novelist," in *Edwardians and Late Victorians*, ed. Richard Ellmann, English Institute Essays: 1959 (New York, 1960), p. 158.

[8] "Technique as Discovery," in *Forms of Modern Fiction*, ed. William Van O'Connor (Minneapolis, 1948), p. 17.

[9] Bergonzi, p. xxiii.

In general terms, my answer will be that George Ponderevo's "private" story concerns a crisis and conversion that make him attempt to purge his consciousness of the delusions and maladies of the existing social order so that, as he writes, he is in the process of becoming what Wells would have us believe is a man of the future. To represent the experiences that induced his quest for salvation, Ponderevo borrows some ready-made forms and languages, including those of the "Condition of England novel," religious confession, and fictional autobiography. But "the spirit of truth-telling" (p. 12) in which he writes requires that the controlling perspective of his book should be that of his renovated consciousness, and this in turn requires a new language and a new form for which he can find no models. Thus the essential and unifying form of *Tono-Bungay* becomes that of a search for expression which inheres in the process of composition itself.

The opening and concluding chapters of the novel establish the priority and the direction of that quest. In both, Ponderevo begins by confidently describing the structure of his novel as the structure of his social experience, in linear and progressive metaphors: the "social trajectory" (p. 10) of his uncle's career and his own, the stages of a journey down the Thames (p. 312), the successive movements of an imaginary "London symphony" (p. 314). Thus the "main line" of his narrative is that of any nineteenth-century "panoramic" novel, leading toward a broad historical vision of English society. In both chapters, however, Ponderevo ends by dismissing these metaphors and, indeed, the very form, substance, and language of his novel as hopelessly inadequate to tell the truth he wishes to tell about "Life—as one man has found it . . . *myself*, and my impressions of the thing as a whole" (p. 11). His deepest intuitions are of a still unrealized reality that cannot be revealed through personal and social history or conveyed in ordinary language: "I have figured it in my last section by the symbol of my destroyer, stark and swift, irrelevant to most human interests. Sometimes I call this reality Science, sometimes I call it Truth" (pp. 316–17). But not even symbol and abstraction can articulate the "something, a quality, an element" that seems to him to be "the heart of life," and he lapses at last into "thought that was nearly formless, into doubts and dreams that have no words" (p. 317).

In this way Wells's narrator himself points to an apparent incoherence in the novel, a disjunction between the import and

structure of the story and the controlling perspective that makes
that story, in one of the narrator's key words, "irrelevant." For
Schorer, this disjunction constitutes the most damaging weakness
of *Tono-Bungay*:

> The novel ends in a kind of meditative rhapsody which denies
> every value that the book had been aiming toward. For of all the
> kinds of social waste which Wells has been describing, this is the
> most inclusive, the final waste. Thus he gives us in the end not a
> novel, but a hypothesis; not an individual destiny, but a theory of
> the future; and not his theory of the future, but a nihilistic vision
> quite opposite from everything that he meant to represent.[10]

David Lodge's argument that the narrator's celebration of his
futuristic destroyer is "ironically double-edged" [11] does not
answer Schorer's objection, since it merely locates the same
disjunction in another aspect of the novel: between the normal
function of Ponderevo as a reliable narrator (in Wayne Booth's
sense) and his putative function in some passages as a foil for the
more humane attitudes of the implied author. But both Schorer
and Lodge are demonstrably wrong in supposing that Wells at
the time he wrote *Tono-Bungay* could not have intended Ponderevo's "hidden mission" in the destroyer to imply what it seems to
imply—a belief that war can foster a vital principle that
counteracts social waste or decay. In *First and Last Things* (1908),
written more or less concurrently with *Tono-Bungay*, Wells
unequivocally declares his belief that "in many ways war is the
most socialistic of all forces. In many ways military organisation
is the most peaceful of activities." [12] Although he hopes that
eventually the development of collective consciousness and a
world commonwealth will eliminate the need for war, he sees it
as "a necessary phase in human and indeed in all animal
development." This is so because "that violence and killing
which between animals of the same species is private and
individual becomes socialised in war. It is a co-operation for
killing that carries with it also a co-operation for saving and a
great development of mutual help and development within the
war-making group" (p. 217).

---

[10] "Technique as Discovery," p. 17.

[11] "*Tono-Bungay* and the Condition of England," p. 242.

[12] *First and Last Things: A Confession of Faith and a Rule of Life* (New York, 1908),
p. 214.

The "metaphysic," as Wells calls it, that supposedly justifies his view of war is all too lucidly expounded in *First and Last Things*. His exposition is worth quoting at length because it provides a convenient summary of the ideal of collective consciousness that informs *Tono-Bungay* from beginning to end. Its bearing on Schorer's view of the novel, moreover, is direct and important. Given Wells's belief, proclaimed here, in the illusoriness of "separate individuality," he can scarcely be expected to have shared the traditional novelistic concern with "individual destiny":

> *The essential fact in man's history* to my sense is the slow unfolding of a sense of community with his kind, of the possibilities of co-operations leading to scarce-dreamt-of collective powers, of a synthesis of the species, of the development of a common general idea, a common general purpose out of a present confusion. In that awakening of the species, one's own personal being lives and moves—a part of it and contributing to it. *One's individual existence is not so entirely cut off as it seems at first; one's entirely separate individuality is another, a profounder, among the subtle inherent delusions of the human mind.* Between you and me as we set our minds together, and between us and the rest of mankind, there is *something*, something real, something that rises through us and is neither you nor me. . . . We, you and I, are not only parts in a thought process, but parts of one flow of blood and life. . . .
>
> I see myself in life as part of a great physical being that strains and I believe grows towards Beauty, and of a great mental being that strains and I believe grows towards knowledge and power. . . . In it I find both concentration of myself and escape from myself, in a word, I find *Salvation*. (pp. 92–95)

This quasi-religious collectivism is in effect the faith through which George Ponderevo ultimately seeks his salvation. His conversion, however, is slow and painful, since he must experience directly the disintegrativeness of separate selfhood in romantic love, personal ambition, and, finally, that "private and individual" violence which, according to *First and Last Things*, "becomes socialised in war." That experience, understood in the context of general social decay, the "hypertrophy" of the Bladesover system, is represented in different parts of the novel in the style of Dickens, Balzac, Conrad, or any other novelist whose vision may have seemed to Wells to have encompassed a particular phase of his narrator's errors and disillusionment. But, from his retrospective point of view, Ponderevo can also see in his past self nascent intuitions of the "one flow of blood and life" that makes the individualist vision of these exemplary novelists, even as embodied in their critical and diagnostic language, finally "irrelevant." Lodge has argued that the principle of coherence in the novel emerges from those passages in which Wells makes use of such language, an imagery of disease and decay derived mainly from Dickens. It seems to me, on the contrary, that Ponderevo's fluent proliferation of diagnostic images, however "charged with imaginative energy," [13] is for him evidence that he has not yet achieved the transformation of consciousness he seeks: "It may be I see decay all about me because I am, in a sense, decay" (p. 311). But the self which perceives and hence *is* decay is a false self which he must destroy in the interest of a potential true and collective self. That potentiality, latent in his intuitions of "something real," provides a kind of notional coherence for the novel which transcends its actual yet ultimately deceptive form and language.

The first phase of Ponderevo's conversion comes after his parting from his wife, Marion:

> As I regard it all now in this retrospect, it seems to me as if in those days of disgust and abandoned aims I discovered myself for the first time. . . .
>
> There were moments when I thought of suicide. . . . I had what the old theologians call a "conviction of sin." I sought salvation—not perhaps in the formulæ a Methodist preacher would recognise—but salvation nevertheless. . . .
>
> In the end of this particular crisis of which I tell so badly, I idealised Science. I decided that in power and knowledge lay the salvation of my life, the secret that would fill my need; that to these things I would give myself. (pp. 164–65)

[13] Lodge, p. 215. Lodge notes the narrator's struggle in this episode "to give definition to a half-apprehended *something*" (p. 238), a negative principle that accounts alike for physical and social decay. But he does not relate this perception to the similar reiterations of the word "something" in Ponderevo's attempts to define the creative principle he later apprehends or see the importance to the novel as a whole of the narrator's quest for expression. What is implied in the opposition of elemental creation and destruction is perhaps a kind of "Manicheism," a term which, in the *Experiment in Autobiography* (p. 576), Wells applies to his now-repudiated phase of "religiosity."

Ponderevo does not yet see that science is merely one expression of the suprahuman processes to which he will later submit himself. Nevertheless, he has already begun to sense the possibility of finding himself by transcending his personal humanity, or by killing it. He rejects socialism as a path to salvation because existing socialist organizations are "a little bit too human, too set about with personalities and foolishness" (p. 165). Even in his love for Marion he has glimpsed an austere impersonal beauty, like that of his destroyer, of which she is the "unconscious custodian" despite the triviality of her "superficial self" (p. 97). Later, in his love-making with Beatrice Normandy, he will come much closer to "the elemental thing" (p. 242), a breaking down of "the boundaries of self" which, according to *First and Last Things* (p. 291), is the purpose of love within the evolving "synthesis of the species."

Like Marion, however, Beatrice is finally unable to overcome the limits of her personal and social self. Moreover, she stirs up in George all those aspirations to personal fulfillment which are also inherent in his uncle's ambition to become the "Napoleon" of commerce (p. 216). Hence, under her influence, he implicates himself still more deeply in his uncle's affairs, in the sickness of economic individualism. At the same time she brings him to a pitch of delusory self-consciousness that gives his life "the quality of stage scenery" (p. 242). What finally reduces his love story to "irrelevance," however, is that in the absence of any relation to collective processes, his passion has no meaning "except itself":

> Love, like everything else in this immense process of social disorganisation in which we live, is a thing adrift, a fruitless thing broken away from its connections. I tell of this love-affair here because of its irrelevance, because it is so remarkable that it should mean nothing, and be nothing except itself. (pp. 303-304)

"Irrelevance" is, as I have suggested, a key word in the novel. The symbolic destroyer is "irrelevant to most human interests" because it is relevant only to the collective interests Ponderevo has begun to pursue; and the personal experience of isolated individuals, thought to be universally human, becomes irrelevant to him. It is in this sense that the murder of the black man on the quap island remains for Ponderevo "the most incidental thing" in his life, as he declares on the first page of the novel, even though at the end he is still haunted by memories of "dead negroes and pestilential swamps" (p. 301). What makes violence, like love, "unmeaning and purposeless" (p. 271) yet, as the same time, "a humiliating self-revelation" (p. 260) is Ponderevo's discovery of the overwhelming power of his own noncollective emotions and, more generally, of man's instinctual nature, a kind of secular original sin.

The expedition to the quap island is an appropriately Conradian journey into "undisciplined nature" and the racial past.[14] A curiously medieval sense of analogy between man's inner world, human society, and the physical universe informs the entire episode. As has been shown, the quap island is a symbolic epitome of England in its disintegration by investment capitalism.[15] At the same time, Ponderevo discovers in the radioactive quap a principle of decay that mirrors the purposeless violence within: "I hated all humanity during the time that the quap was near me" (p. 270). He fears that the principle of the quap, and of his own human nature, may be that of the universe itself and that consequently the world is evolving to "no splendid climax and finale, no towering accumulation of achievements but just—atomic decay" (p. 268).

Ponderevo associates his vision of his dead victim with a dream in which he had seen his Uncle Teddy with a slash in his throat from which there exudes an ochreous quap-like substance; and he is unable to dismiss a "horrible obsession" that the face in the dream and the putrescent body are one thing, "acutely alive and perceiving" (p. 273), which he has attempted but failed to kill. What he half-consciously desires to kill in Uncle Teddy is what seems to remain alive in the black man and in himself: human nature in its disintegrating condition of isolated consciousness. In a later episode, when Uncle Teddy's inner being has been revealed in the delirium of his last illness, Ponderevo reflects that "all things unspoken in our souls partake somewhat of the laxity of delirium and dementia" (p. 294). The only means of escaping such delirium is to deny absolutely the authority of the isolated self by affirming faith in "something that is at once human

---

[14] Bergonzi (pp. xxvi–xxviii) provides a full analysis of Conradian echoes in the quap episode.
[15] Lodge, pp. 215, 219.

achievement and the most inhuman of existing things"—the
austere abstraction evolving "out of the heart of life" (pp. 316,
317).

Thus when Ponderevo sails down the Thames in his destroyer,
he is not, as Schorer has argued, denying but rather affirming
"every value that the book had been aiming toward." His aim in
building the destroyer, the "X2," is to transcend individual,
instinctive violence through collective violence, in the service of a
still unidentified revolutionary community that may come into
being. Appalled though one may be by such a revolution, the X2
is the antagonist and not, as Lodge suggests, the symbolic
equivalent of Xk, the unidentified destructive element in quap,
since it stands for a competing principle of elemental reality,
the creative principle in which Ponderevo places his desperate
faith.

Clearly, then, Ponderevo's personal story is of a piece with his
view of social history as it is embodied in his commentary on the
Bladesover system and in his account of the career of Teddy
Ponderevo. The ideology he seeks to overturn through his
doctrine of salvation is, in effect, Uncle Teddy's faith in the
"romance of modern commerce" (p. 124), of which his friend
Ewart ironically remarks: " 'It's mercy—it's salvation' " (p. 131).
It is important to observe that Uncle Teddy's success in creating
faith in his patent medicines and investment schemes stems
mainly from his powers of language. He sees himself as a kind of
artist in advertising slogans, and advertising is a disease of
language in just the sense that investment capitalism is the
cancer in the Bladesover system. I am reminded here of
Wittgenstein's aphorism: "Philosophy is a battle against the
bewitchment of our intelligence by means of language." [16] To his
uncle's verbal conjuring, George opposes "the fine realities of
steel" (p. 10).

It is in this connection that the narrative language of
Tono-Bungay becomes a subject as well as the medium of the book.
Ponderevo is not, he insists, a master of language. His true
medium is "turbine machines and boat-building" (p. 12); and he
is suspicious of all artful uses of words, since language is the main
means by which the illusions of existing society and individual

[16] *Philosophical Investigations*, trans. G. E. M. Anscombe (Oxford, 1967), § 109.

consciousness have been perpetuated. This would seem to be the main reason that Wells chose to invent a nonliterary persona to serve as his narrator, an "objective-minded person" (p. 247), as Ponderevo calls himself. If he is to emerge from the illusions of a verbal culture, the potential man of the future must be relatively invulnerable to "the bewitchment of our intelligence by means of language." Nevertheless, he must struggle for expression, for he must bring to the surface and expose the "things unspoken in our souls," the dementia of subjectivity by which, as a man of his time and place, he knows himself to be affected.

For this reason, among others, Ponderevo finds it necessary to tell his love story as fully as he can, even though it is "quite the most difficult part of my story to write" (p. 247). In part this is so because he lacks literary models: "No one has ever yet dared to tell a love-story completely, its alternations, its comings and goings, its debased moments, its hate" (p. 248). More important, the impersonal "elemental thing" he has known with Beatrice endures in his new consciousness and is still more difficult to put into words. Here, of course, is his main task as a writer. New truths require a new language. As he and his destroyer "tear into the great spaces of the future," it seems to him that "the turbines fall to talking in unfamiliar tongues" (p. 316). But he cannot translate their message, or find a verbal equivalent for the single clear note that sounds through the confusions of his "London symphony." He asks: "How can I express the values of a thing at once so essential and so immaterial?" (p. 316). Meanwhile, still preoccupied with the diseases of language, he remembers how before his departure the newspaper reporters had told his story in "turgid degenerate Kiplingese" (p. 317). Clearly that was another story.

Ponderevo's problem is one that D. H. Lawrence described as the central one of his time in an undated essay published posthumously in *Phoenix*:

> This is our true bondage. This is the agony of our human existence, that we can only feel things in conventional feeling-patterns. Because when these feeling-patterns become inadequate, when they will no longer body forth the workings of the yeasty soul, then we are in torture. It is like a deaf-mute trying to speak. Something is inadequate in the expression-apparatus, and we hear strange howlings. So we are now howling inarticulate,

because what is yeastily working in us has no voice and no language.[17]

Lawrence, too, is seeking a man of the future, though he would have rejected the Wellsian version:

> Where is the new baby of a new conception of life? Who feels him kicking in the womb of time?
>
> Nobody! Nobody! Not even the Socialists and Bolshevists themselves. Not the Buddhists, nor the Christian Scientists, nor the scientists, nor the Christians . . . a revolution is really the birth of a new baby, a new idea, a new feeling, a new way of feeling, a new feeling-pattern. It is the birth of a new man.[18]

It is not surprising, then, that the young Lawrence should have found *Tono-Bungay*, when he read it in the *English Review*, to be "a great book." [19] Many of Wells's preoccupations at the time he was writing *Tono-Bungay* would also absorb Lawrence a few years later. An anonymous review of *Sons and Lovers* described its theme in precisely the terms of Ponderevo's summary of his story at the beginning of the last chapter: "I have called it *Tono-Bungay*, but I had far better have called it *Waste*" (p. 311). The reviewer writes: "The ruling idea in the book is the pitiful wastage of the best in men and women," and later, "The idea of waste still rules the story." Another comment by the reviewer suggests the sense in which Lawrence became the novelist Wells failed to become in the love episodes of *Tono-Bungay* and, soon after, in *Ann Veronica* (1909): "We know of no active English novelist—today—who has Mr. Lawrence's power to put into words the rise and fall of passion." [20]

.The Rainbow, of course, answers point for point Ponderevo's appeal for an example of how "to tell a love story completely." And Lawrence's constantly quoted letter to Edward Garnett[21] on his effort to transcend "the old stable *ego*—of the character" reveals a concern with discovering an impersonal or suprapersonal principle in human beings that brings to mind Ponderevo's

---

[17] ["The Good Man"], *Phoenix: The Posthumous Papers of D. H. Lawrence*, ed. Edward D. McDonald (New York, 1936), p. 753.

[18] *Ibid.*, pp. 753–54.

[19] *Collected Letters of D. H. Lawrence*, ed. Harry T. Moore (New York, 1962), I, 54.

[20] *Saturday Review*, June 21, 1913, pp. 780–81.

[21] *Collected Letters*, I, 281–83.

interest in what Marion is when she is "released, as it were, from herself": "I don't so much care about what the woman *feels*—in the ordinary usage of the word. . . . I only care about what the woman *is* . . . what she *is* as a phenomenon (or as representing some greater, inhuman will), instead of what she feels according to the human conception." The immediate stimulus of his interest in "that which is physic—non-human, in humanity," Lawrence told Garnett, was a reading of Marinetti (presumably the "Technical Manifesto of Futurist Literature"),[22] and the conclusion of *Tono-Bungay* also reflects the spirit of the times that produced Futurism and similar *avant-garde* attempts to transcend the Nietzschean "human, all too human." [23] Indeed, Wells is generally regarded as one of Marinetti's main predecessors in preaching the beauty of the machine.[24] Though Lawrence shared their interest in suprahuman forces and qualities, he objected, as one would expect, to the cult of Science and the machine: "I agree with them about the weary sickness of pedantry and tradition and inertness, but I don't agree with them as to the cure and the escape. They will progress down the purely male or intellectual or scientific line." [25] His objections would surely have applied to "the cure and the escape" proposed in *Tono-Bungay*. In a review of *The World of William Clissold*, Lawrence expressed another point of disagreement with Wells:

> We wonder that he so insists on the Universal or racial *mind* of man, as the only hope of salvation . . . is it not obvious that without a full and subtle emotional life the mind itself must wither: or that it must turn itself into an automatic sort of grind-mill, grinding upon itself? [26]

One notes, however, that the word Lawrence emphasizes is "mind," not "Universal" or "racial." For both writers sought

[22] *Ibid.,* pp. 279–80. See F. T. Marinetti, ed., *I manifesti del futurismo* (Florence, 1914), pp. 88–96. One cannot help wondering whether Marinetti's use, in several contexts, of symbolic destroyers was suggested by *Tono-Bungay*, since Marinetti was in London in 1910 and again early in 1912, knew English, and might well have read Wells's novel.

[23] Bergonzi, pp. xix–xx.

[24] See Marianne W. Martin, *Futurist Art and Theory* (Oxford, 1968), p. 42 and n. 2.

[25] *Collected Letters*, I, 280.

[26] *Phoenix*, p. 349.

salvation in a quasi-religious sense by distinguishing "true individuality" from "separate individuality" and attempting to define a realm of unity beyond the divisions of existing society and the self-conscious self. The following is a characteristic Lawrentian formulation of this idea:

> Paradoxical as it may sound, the individual is only truly himself when he is unconscious of his own individuality, when he is unaware of his own isolation, when he is not split into subjective and objective, when there is no *me or you*, no *me or it* in his consciousness, but the *me and you*, the *me and it* is a living *continuum*, as if all were connected by a living membrane.[27]

For Lawrence as for Wells, finally, the penalty for disrupting the living continuum of consciousness was the decay and sickness he also found in man and society. In *The Rainbow* especially Lawrence uses a system of elemental images to indicate qualities of being beneath or beyond the personal self, and his imagery of decay has much the same implication as Wells's. The obvious difference is that Lawrence is concerned with the condition of England mainly as it is reflected in the condition of the English soul. Ursula Brangwen sees her Uncle Tom, the pit manager, and her former schoolmistress, Winifred Inger, in a way that recalls George Ponderevo's vision of Uncle Teddy, the quap, and the black man's corpse:

> She saw gross, ugly movements in her mistress, she saw a clayey, inert, unquickened flesh, that reminded her of the great prehistoric lizards. . . . He too had something marshy about him—the succulent moistness and turgidity, and the same brackish, nauseating effect of a marsh, where life and decaying are one. . . . Their marshy, bitter-sweet corruption came sick and unwholesome in her nostrils. Anything, to get out of the fœtid air. She would leave . . . their strange, soft, half-corrupt element.[28]

What these and other points of affinity add up to, it should be clear, is not a demonstration of total kinship or of direct influence, but rather of essential contemporaneity, though Lawrence may have shaped some of his convictions in opposition to those of Wells, opposition being true friendship. Lawrence and

[27] *Ibid.*, p. 761.
[28] *The Rainbow* (New York, 1961), p. 350

Wells were responding in their own ways to a similar inheritance from the past and a similar orientation in present circumstances: the organicist and deterministic theories of the nineteenth century, the pervasive awareness among intellectuals of their time of social disintegration and personal isolation, the apocalyptic mood of the years before the First World War, their own lower-class origins and hostility toward middle-class values, and their common distaste for the self-consciously artful and introspective fiction of James and Conrad. But even Virginia Woolf, who regarded herself as a literary antagonist of both Wells and Lawrence, shared some of their common preoccupations. In *To the Lighthouse*, for example, her privileged characters also seek to transcend the imprisoning ego and to become "one" with impersonal forces. In her criticism she articulated the need that Lawrence keenly felt and Wells expressed through George Ponderevo to invent new uses of language that might reflect or create a new mode of awareness in modern man—though it was not the same mode she had in mind.[29] This concern is reflected in the narrative framework of *To the Lighthouse*: Lily Briscoe's effort to paint a picture that will embody her vision of the Ramsays and of the symbolic setting of their lives. The quest for expression becomes the unifying form of the novel, as it is in *Tono-Bungay*.

Tono-Bungay is only incipiently and in its largest but vaguest outlines an experimental novel in the sense in which the term applies to *The Rainbow* and *To the Lighthouse*. Its obvious method is to assimilate through thematic and stylistic imitation the points of view of certain nineteenth-century novelists, since ultimately Wells failed to develop an equally powerful way of telling his own kind of truth. But if, as I have argued, the controlling perspective is the one the narrator asserts it to be and the one that is implicit in the whole of his personal story, then Wells was either wrong or disingenuous when he insisted that *Tono-Bungay* was conceived "upon the accepted lines." The relation of the novel to *First and Last Things*, a book which Wells later drastically revised and which he did not allude to in the *Experiment in Autobiography*, would seem to confirm my view.[30] George Pon-

[29] See, for example, "The Narrow Bridge of Art," *Collected Essays*, ed. Leonard Woolf (London, 1966), II, 218–19.

[30] The revised edition (London, 1917) omits the glorification of war and military organization found in the original version. Much later, *First and Last*

derevo is made to say that he is writing "a novel, not a treatise," and that he is still seeking, not proclaiming, the "something" through which he may attain "the utter redemption of myself" (p. 167). But clearly what he is seeking is the faith Wells thought he had found when he wrote a treatise in his own person.

What gives *Tono-Bungay* its special interest for the study of early modern fiction is that in it one finds the representation of a process by which some characteristic themes and techniques of the nineteenth-century novel become "irrelevant" to the expressive needs of the narrator. The place where that process occurs is where Lawrence, Woolf, and others found it to be—within a consciousness that is attempting to discard "the old stable *ego*" along with its confidence in existing social values and searching for an impersonal principle to purify the self of "the taint of personality," to use a phrase from Meredith's poem, "The Lark Ascending." What results is an interest in "elemental realities," qualities of life, process and being, rather than traits of character displayed in behavior or the flow of consciousness as it creates or responds to behavior. To suggest that *Tono-Bungay* is in this sense a modern novel is not, however, to imply that it is better than its critics have thought—only more original and perhaps historically more important. Wells's use of a narrator who is a (relatively) inarticulate engineer does not finally compensate, in my opinion, for the crudity of feeling and infelicity of language that mark passage after passage. These are defects of Wells's own "mental texture," as he put it,[31] and they are defects of his novel.

I should like to suggest, though a little reluctantly, that the issue here extends beyond matters of technique or even quality of mind to the troublesome and perhaps unresolvable question of the relation between literature and belief. My reading of *Tono-Bungay* reveals an underlying attitude which I find to be

---

Things was "replaced," as Wells stated in the introduction, by *The Conquest of Time* (London, 1942), in which he stripped away the whole religious framework and vocabulary of the earlier book, retaining little of the original argument beyond the view that "the life of the species as a whole" is "far greater than the individual life" (p. 35). Thus Wells's insistence in the 1920s and after on the traditional form and sociological substance of *Tono-Bungay* probably reflects, in part at least, his repudiation of his former belief in salvation through submission to suprahuman processes.

[31] *Experiment in Autobiography*, p. 14.

morally vicious. It seems to me that the implications of the "ambiguous symbol" of the destroyer[32] and indeed of the whole narrative framework are far from ambiguous, though they are not necessarily very clear. The value of human life lies in the achievement of collective and suprahuman aims. Individual persons are "irrelevant" except in their relation to such aims, even while the ultimate purposes of the impersonal force remain unknown, marked by an "X." I should like to believe that Ponderevo is an unreliable narrator, that we must see him ironically as a victim of the social disorders he diagnoses, but I can find no internal or external evidence to support such a view, except in so far as Wells himself may be seen as a victim of those disorders. Ponderevo is ambivalent, true enough, in his feelings about some of the characters. He continues to love and admire Beatrice Normandy, his Aunt Susan, even Uncle Teddy. But he turns away from these people because they belong to the "unreal" part of his experience, because his love for them is "torn away from its connections" and has no meaning beyond itself. Though Wells in *First and Last Things* celebrated personal love as "the individualised correlative of Salvation" (p. 292), he also asserted that it must remain subordinate to "the synthesis of a collective will in humanity" (p. 143). And hatred, from this point of view, "must be in its nature a good thing" because "we individuals exist as such . . . for the Purpose in things, and our separations and antagonisms serve that Purpose" (p. 143).

It would be easy enough, in reaching a critical judgment of *Tono-Bungay*, to put aside the moral issue. If the form and language of the novel are designed, as I think they are, to create in the reader an imaginative participation in Ponderevo's conversion, one can argue that the novel fails in what it attempts, that only the negative criticism of society, the panoramic view, is presented with sufficient energy and precision of language to elicit a vivid response. For this very reason, however, it is important to see that the essential character of Wells's novel does not reside in its element of imaginative energy, that it is a failed experiment in a fictional mode that Lawrence practiced, in *The Rainbow* and after, with infinitely greater delicacy of perception, artfulness of language, and rhetorical success: the kind of novel

[32] Bergonzi, p. xix.

that by representing the processes of elemental consciousness attempts to transform the reader's conception of what consciousness is and consequently to change his mode of awareness. The new consciousness of the ideal Lawrentian reader must embrace not only a belief in the suprahuman forces, known through sexual experience, through which his characters seek salvation, but also hatred and contempt for whatever in human personality was hateful to Lawrence at any given time: the loathsome marshy quality, for example, that defines his middle-class characters in *The Rainbow*. If one feels, as I do, that such purposes are evil, ought one to affirm that the language and form of Lawrence's novels are aesthetically defensible even though the ends they serve—assuming that they are in fact served—are morally and psychologically destructive?

I cannot answer this question; but when I read *Tono-Bungay*, it occurs to me that there may, after all, be one clear connection between literature and belief. All too often we are bewitched by language, not necessarily into unwilling conversion, but rather into willful blindness: a refusal to understand what we do not wish to believe. Such bewitchment may well have affected some critics of Lawrence's novels; I cannot examine this question here. It has, I believe, seriously distorted many readings of *Tono-Bungay*, including, perhaps, this one. But to read Wells's novel as though it were written in the vein of Balzac or Dickens or any other nineteenth-century novelist seems to me a disservice to those authors and ultimately to Wells himself. *Tono-Bungay* is an original and unified novel that distinguishes and reflects with remarkable percipience a newly emerging spirit—it may have been an evil one—of the age in which its author lived and wrote.

Through the Novelist's Looking-Glass

by Gloria Glikin Fromm

During more than half a century as a writer of fiction, H. G. Wells was a tireless—and protesting—autobiographer. He deplored the practice of "reading between the lines" of his books. He demanded that people accept a novel of his as "nothing but a novel" instead of trying to "squint through" it, looking for the author. Yet he left so many portraits of himself in his fictional characters that no one has had the temerity even to collate them. Indeed to try to see him through his own mirror is to be faced with several images at once; and each of these—the journalist, the prophet, the scientist *manqué,* the unwitting artist—was offered up again in 1966, during the centennial celebration of his birth, as the real H. G. Wells. But if we want to grasp the protean Wells, the man beneath the various shapes he seemed compelled to assume, we cannot ignore the mirror held up to him by his close friend and reader, the novelist Dorothy Richardson. In her long serial-novel *Pilgrimage*, recently republished, is a brilliant full-length portrait of Wells under the guise of fiction. Few have noticed the portrait or troubled to take it into account, even though Wells himself acknowledged it. Now that *Pilgrimage* has been made available once again, Miss Richardson may be recognized as Wells's most authoritative "biographer" thus far. She provides us in any case with a second looking-glass into Wells which makes his own seem much less crowded and forbidding.

He certainly did all he could both to multiply his likeness and to discourage autobiographical reading. The less his readers knew him, he once scoffed, the more certain they were to discover

"Through the Novelist's Looking Glass" by Gloria Glikin Fromm. From *Kenyon Review* 31 (1969). Reprinted by permission of the author.

him in his characters (and then to charge him with inconsistency because the opinions of his heroes varied "scandalously" from book to book). Of course his major characters resembled him, he pointed out: "how can one imagine and invent the whole interior world of an uncongenial type?" But if he wished to write "a mental autobiography instead of a novel," Wells argued, he would not hesitate to do so—and to reveal his mind in full.

In his *Experiment in Autobiography*, published in 1934, six years after these remarks, Wells revealed—along with an undeniable inconsistency and some striking shifts of emphasis—that he usually meant *mind* even when he suggested *self.* He gave his book a modest subtitle: "the discoveries and conclusions of a very ordinary brain." Then he warned his readers that he would not be able to avert "egoism." He was being his "own rabbit," he said; he could "find no other specimen so convenient for dissection." But Wells failed to take himself apart not merely because he was intent upon studying the growth of his ideas. Despite its analytic framework, his extraordinary book is largely a collection of the self-portraits he had already drawn in his novels. He could not refrain, in the end, from treating himself as if he were a series of characters of his own making. He did not confront but rather transformed himself—as autobiographers are more than likely to do.

Wells had developed the habit of fictionalizing himself through more than thirty years of novel writing. From the start, in *Love and Mr. Lewisham* (1900), many of his central characters were thinly disguised, sometimes comic versions of Wells. Indeed his novel *Marriage* (1912) caught the interest of a careful reader such as Henry James not for the "story" of the characters Wells created but for the story of Wells the author: "I see you 'behave' all along much more than I see them . . ." James wrote to Wells, "so that the ground of the drama is somehow most of all in the adventure for *you*—not to say *of* you. . . ." James's critical point, evident in this letter, was the fictional unreality of Wells's people and their lives. Quoting from the letter in his autobiography, Wells maintained that James's ideal—"the novel of completely consistent characterization . . . painted deep and round and solid"—was not the only kind possible. He regretted, moreover, that he had been unable to answer James in 1912 as he could now, after twenty-two years. Then he had conceded that his "so-called novels were artless self-revelatory stuff." Now, in 1934, he was convinced that biography could not be avoided. Unlike James, who objected, he said, to "the idea that there was a biographical element in any good novel," Wells approved of the idea—and carried it still further. He insisted it was "beyond the power of man to 'create' individuals absolutely. . . . Every 'living' character in a novel is drawn, frankly or furtively, from life." As a matter of fact, Wells had come to believe that if biography could be written "all out," novels would cease to be read.

In the majority of his own novels, containing what he called "written discussions of living people," Wells tried to approximate biography and "autobiography." He turned into fiction not only many aspects of his personality but also the circumstances and experiences of his life. In some of his novels, he went so far as to imagine what he would have become under slightly different conditions or with less intelligence and determination. The heroes of these novels shared Wells's abiding concern: the state of the world, and one man's power to improve it. They were also engaged in trying to understand their lives—if not their personal failures—by means of "truthful comment" about themselves as well as others. This freedom to be "searching and outspoken" Wells felt was crucial in order to write biography as he conceived it. But he neglected to note that his heroes shared, in addition, a compelling urge to explain and justify their lives. Furthermore, the urgency with which they told their stories emanated from Wells. The older he grew, the more engrossed he became—as C. P. Snow has remarked—in "rationalising his own life." Nearly all the work of Wells's middle and late years carries this burden, underlying his repeated choice of the first-person narrative method. He thought he preferred the autobiographical form in fiction because of the freedom it would grant. In effect, however, it allowed him to work his will freely on the materials of himself—with the paradoxical result James had observed: Wells's characters, endowed with his own vigorous life, are not self-sustaining. Instead they are bound to Wells and constrained by the very liberty he needed to produce them. The astute James had penetrated to the truth that Wells's fullest creative energies were deflected inward.

Under these circumstances—with so many of his characters mirroring the diverse ways in which Wells saw himself, mocked himself, vindicated himself—the writing of his "real" autobiography must have led him into a curious, though unperceived dilemma: how was he to separate the fictional characters he had created as projections of himself from the splendidly live, prolific nature he had grown used to converting into fiction?

Wells did not solve a problem he scarcely knew existed. He merely went on doing what he had always done in his novels—portraying himself from different vantage points, according to the angle of the mirror into which he looked. Sometimes it reflected the shy, awkward young man he had been. At other times, it showed the scientist he had wished to be, or the "prophet," the champion of "free love," and the "citizen of the world" he had become. In each of his novels, one of these images of himself predominated. But in his autobiography, unable or unwilling to decide which he really preferred, Wells projected them all. When added to the self-portraits abounding in his novels, they reveal Wells as the provocative and puzzling figure Dorothy Richardson undertook to fathom.

The mirror she held up to Wells in her sequence-novel *Pilgrimage* enables us to bring into focus his views of himself, and to see that underlying them is one thematic self not entirely known to him but recurring with subtle variations throughout his novels: the timid, endearing little man who suddenly exerts his will in a dual attempt to transform his life and reform the world. As nearly all artists do, Wells unconsciously plumbed the depths of his own being, producing a series of characters who reflect their creator's most deeply embedded image of himself. Dorothy Richardson helps to pluck this image out.

Her friendship with Wells—the first writer she had ever met—began in 1896. At this time, Dorothy Richardson had no thought of a career in literature. But during the next ten years, encouraged by Wells and others, she turned to writing; and found the autobiographical impulse as strong in her as it was in Wells. For her, however, fiction came to be more consciously a medium of self-revelation; indeed—as it never did for Wells— fiction grew for Dorothy Richardson into both the record and the instrument of self-discovery. The novel she set about writing in 1912 (and then published in parts between 1915 and 1938) was to be a full though disguised and subjective account of her life, leading up to the point at which she began *Pilgrimage*. In such a work—given his relationship with her—H. G. Wells would have to play the role of a major character.

She cast herself as Miriam Henderson, a girl of the late-Victorian era who comes to London the same year she had come, to take the position she had held in the office of several young dentists. When almost immediately Miriam visits an old school friend (as Dorothy Richardson did) and is introduced to her writer-husband, Hypo G. Wilson (the G, according to Hypo's wife, stands for God), we begin to recognize H. G. Wells behind the fictional name bearing the initials of his own. *Hypo,* as the "fixing" agent in the development of a picture and the cleansing solution in dental laboratories, suits the role Wilson plays in *Pilgrimage*. His personal relationship with Miriam develops into a struggle between two minds that steadily diverge; between two people who ultimately come together and then part; and between two strong wills that fight for domination.

The drama of their relationship unfolds in *Pilgrimage*, with Hypo Wilson's square-shaped figure of fact and fictional guise taking form through the medium of Miriam's consciousness. Hers is the single point of view in the novel. It is reported in a third-person narrative that functions in part as a means of concealment, corresponding to the fictional mask given to Wells. A reader warned beforehand, however, would be able to identify Wells and Dorothy Richardson with relative ease. Indeed Wells admitted in his autobiography that he was Wilson. He remarked that the description of his life at home in Surrey when Dorothy Richardson first began to visit him had an "astonishing accuracy." But not a single contemporary reviewer of any of Dorothy Richardson's volumes noted the presence of Wells in her work. She deliberately mentioned him in *Pilgrimage* to keep Wilson's identity from the general public. A more effective device than this was her portrayal of Wilson and Miriam as complete characters in a fictional world. They are not photographic reproductions. Nor do their experiences parallel in every detail those of Miss Richardson and Wells. On the contrary, they are telescoped and shaped in order to give artistic life to a reality that itself underwent the subtle changes wrought by memory and the intervening years. The achievement of Dorothy Richardson, unlike Wells's, lies in her creation of Hypo Wilson as a

self-contained character in fiction at the same time that she
caught the essential qualities of H. G. Wells and of her intimate
relationship with him.

Her portrait of Wells begins in *The Tunnel*, that part of
Pilgrimage he singled out for comment in his autobiography. In
this volume, his fictional self had a charm as well as power that
must have gratified him—but certain aspects, too, that might
well have irritated him. The Wilson introduced to Miriam is
more formidable than the Wells Dorothy Richardson had met
for the first time. Instead of a thirty-year-old man—still slender
and socially awkward—Dorothy Richardson projects the thick-
ening, confident, assertive Wells of the early years of the
twentieth century. She sends her heroine down into the country
to meet "a little fair square man not much taller than she" who
looks reassuringly "like a grocer's assistant" but does not behave
like one. He begins at once to ask questions by making
statements: "You caught the elusive three-fifteen. This is your
bag. We can carry it off without waiting for the . . . British
porter. You've done your journey brilliantly. We haven't far to
walk." Even though he has "a common voice, with a Cockney
twang," it becomes increasingly clear he is by no means an
ordinary man. One would need to be always on guard against
the possibility of a "strange direct attack, pushing through and
out to some unknown place." Wilson's absolute certainty about
everything is distinctly threatening. The books of the future, he
foretells, will eliminate the relationship between men and
women. Science, he insists, is the most important subject of the
present. God, he affirms, was created by man out of his craven
fear of the unknown and his equally craven need for reassurance.
Wilson states facts, not opinions. The young Miriam, convinced
he is wrong, wants him "only to go on"; she feels certain he must
have some kind of secret, a "secret that made him so strong, even
with his weak voice, strong and fascinating."

If Wells in turn had any kind of secret, it seemed to be the
talent evinced in *The Time Machine* that W. E. Henley described
as "unique" and that Wells used unremittingly. He called
himself one of those "adventurous outsiders," like G. B. Shaw, to
whom England was "liable" in his time. As such a man, with no
"predetermined" role to play, he felt he could be "aggressive and

derisive and let persuasion go hang." But in his early life there had been little promise of any mobility at all. He was the grandson of an innkeeper and a gardener, and the son of an unsuccessful, bewildered couple who struggled under the weight of a small china shop in Bromley, Kent. The name of the shop, which his parents had no part in choosing, was Atlas House; in its window stood a figure of the Titan. During nearly his entire adult life, Wells would speak as if he "sustained the whole world upon [his] shoulders." When he was a child, however, Atlas House bore down on Wells as much as on his parents. For a boy of his class, there were few avenues of escape; and he had to contend with poor health to boot. He managed nonetheless to overcome the threat of life as a draper: he read books instead of learning the trade; and secured a "free studentship" at the Normal School of Science in London. But the scientific career he thought was within his grasp eluded him. Almost at the same time that he failed as a student, Wells collapsed with a damaged kidney and a seemingly tubercular lung.

The twenty-one-year-old Wells, five feet five and weighing slightly more than 100 pounds, won out over his physical breakdown by convincing himself on a spring afternoon that he had "died enough." He said in his autobiography, "I stopped dying then and there, and in spite of moments of some provocation, I have never died since."

He met the academic reverse by taking up another career "as compensation." If science was closed to him, he would barge into journalism—and thence to literature. Or so he preferred, later on, to view the move. He would claim in his autobiography that he had set about healing his wounded ego by persuading himself he was "a remarkable wit and potential writer."

By the time Dorothy Richardson met him, he had begun to persuade others, too, that he was a special young man. Within a few years, he had produced a volume of short stories and two longer pieces of fiction (*The Time Machine* and *The Wonderful Visit*); he had written a series of critical articles in the esteemed *Saturday Review*. In these, Wells developed a realistic conception of the novel with the kind of care that belied his assumed indifference to standards and form. At the same time, he was shaping a full-length novel of his own. It would be *Love and Mr. Lewisham*, a witty and documented story of a young man whose

ambition to be a scientist is thwarted. But before finishing
Lewisham, Wells turned to and completed *The Island of Dr. Moreau*,
in which there was no sign of his Cockney assurance or his
humor. In this tale, he offered his vision of human life as a losing
battle with brutish instinct. No matter how painful the process of
developing reason and a moral sense, man could not—he
felt—vanquish the animal in him. He did not believe the
intellect would prevail in spite of the theoretical assumption on
the part of science that it would. Taking the stance of the
prophet he maintained for the rest of his life, Wells issued one of
his first warnings to mankind: in the free growth of the scientific
mind lay potential disaster.

Such was the man whose complex inner and outer life became
entwined with Dorothy Richardson's. While she continued to
work in London, Wells moved from Surrey to Kent, his
self-confidence—and his income—steadily rising. Dorothy Richardson, still visiting the Wellses and beginning to develop her
own views that often clashed with his, absorbed the material she
would later use in the creation of Hypo Wilson. The heroine of
Pilgrimage is exposed to a Wilson at the stage Wells had reached
with the writing of *Anticipations* (1901) and *Mankind in the Making*
(1903). In spite of his fear that man's intellect and his inhumanity might flourish at the same rate, Wells was resolutely
determined upon progress; and his own advancement became
inextricably mingled with the world's. He could not help
translating into universal terms his personal ambition. Nor could
he refrain from haranguing the world—once he had gained its
ear. But he was not content with the platform provided by his
sociological works. He turned again to fiction, with the aim of
stretching it and using it as a medium for his social and political
ideas—and also for self-justification. To him, however, this kind
of fiction represented an enlargement for the good of all. He even
claimed he "was not so much expanding the novel as getting
right out of it"—into what he called biography, the form he
hoped would one day be disburdened of the "subterfuge of
fiction."

Wells's constant theme, expressed as directly as possible, was
that the world could be improved. By exercising "intelligence
and good will," mankind might be able to find its way out of the
morass of wasted life. This firm belief led him to join the Fabian

Society in 1903. In a short time, he was lecturing the Fabians on the mistakes he thought they were making. There came a point at which, as the secretary of the society reported, the question needed to be asked: "Was the Society to be controlled by those who had made it or was it to be handed over to Mr. Wells?" Wells described himself, in relation to both the Socialists and the Feminists, as an *"enfant terrible."* One of his quarrels with the Feminists was that they "repudiated" the importance of "sexual health and happiness," which Wells, finding these essential to his own well-being, had been expounding in lectures and pamphlets and would continue to expound in novels as well as in conversation. Dorothy Richardson listened to his forceful and persuasive arguments. She pondered the question of "free love," observed the irregularities of Wells's personal life (indeed she contributed to them), and in time plunged the heroine of *Pilgrimage* into the midst of Hypo Wilson's plans for a new world.

She endowed Wilson with the exasperating conviction of Wells that all that was "plain" to him should be "plain to everyone." But she also made the loose, tweedy, stocky, abruptly moving figure of Hypo Wilson as attractive and memorable to Miriam as Wells's had been to her. All Wilson's mannerisms sink deep into the consciousness of the observant Miriam—his way of speaking, for example, of making "little short statements, each improving on the one before it and coming out of it, and little subdued snortings [hcna, hcna] at the back of his nose in the pauses between his sentences as if he were afraid of being answered or interrupted before he developed the next thing." Like Wells (whose arguments with George Bernard Shaw in the Fabian Society were feats of mental endurance and contests for supremacy), Wilson demands the entire stage and keeps it by any means at his disposal.

He exacts a great deal more than attention. Dorothy Richardson has her heroine learn that the gratifying interest Wilson shows in her is bound to take the form of an attempt to shape her life. She resists instinctively, but at the same time is anxious to win his approval, to continue to hold his interest by never giving him one of those "dull answers" which seem to baffle him. She is managing to be as "brilliant and amusing" as she immediately saw he required people to be. Yet when he decides she ought to try to write, and insists she bring him a piece of original prose, she rebels. One does not write, she feels, "about anything" at all; nor should one be told to write. Instead of obeying him, she brings on her next visit three short stories translated from the German. He reads them, and points at her a "minatory finger," dismissing them as "gross sentimentality" and branding her as an "admirer of poor stuff." His "brief comprehensive judgment" is delivered in his "high-pitched, colourless, thinking voice." Even though he praises the translation itself as "sleek and clean," he goes on to say contemptuously, "You could make from two to three hundred a year at this sort of thing."

"This sort of thing" is not Hypo Wilson's way. He earns a good deal more money by being unmistakably Wilson, and he knows very well what his own value is in monetary terms. So did Wells, who once complained truculently to Arnold Bennett about not being included in Bennett's book on contemporary fiction, and offered as justification of his complaint the fact that "the *Strand Magazine* pays £125 for a short story by me . . ."

The tone of these remarks by the fictional and the real Wells can be heard in the description of himself offered by Wells in his autobiography. He was "a typical Cockney," he said, who revered no one and felt inferior to nobody. Dorothy Richardson, in effect altering the terms and form of his comment, preferred to show Hypo Wilson convinced of his superiority and determined to be revered. She chose to give evidence, too, of his wish to dominate, illustrating this in his attitude toward the writing Miriam actually brings herself to attempt. When Wilson finds her working on a book review during one of her visits, he is quick to bestow his formula for success: she ought merely to "sniff" at the first page of the book, "glance at the conclusion," and "get [her] three points"; that would "run [her] through a thousand words." Then he proposes to write the review for her. She refuses, boasting she has "fifty ideas," and he retorts, "That's too many, Miriam. That's the trouble with you. . . . You're messing up your mind . . . with too swift a succession of ideas."

Her mind is orderly enough, nonetheless, for the practical-minded Wilson to put it to use. He has her read certain of his own manuscripts, as Wells asked Dorothy Richardson to read his—and sometimes chastised her for overlooking an error. Miriam, on the contrary, never seems to miss anything. Indeed on one occasion she thinks she has managed to turn the tables on Wilson. Looking up from his work, she comments blandly: "You ought to cut out the pathos in that passage." "*Which* passage, Miriametta?" "You weaken the whole argument by coming forward in those three words to tell your readers what they ought to feel. . . ." "Yes. *Which* passage?" "In the moment that the reader turns away everything goes . . ." "Passage, passage———." Wilson is concerned only with identifying the obtrusive words. He made a mistake which she spotted; and he shows no surprise at either her helpfulness or the existence of the error. In the same way, Wells took for granted the innumerable and methodical corrections Arnold Bennett made on the proofs of several books sent to him merely to be read before they were published. Wells knew of his carelessness, accepted it, even took a certain pride in it. His mind, he would claim, was occupied with more vital matters.

Such as socialism. Characteristically, he tried to bring others into the fold—Bennett, for example, who responded by maintaining that Wells could not "make" him a socialist since he was one already. In the same way, Hypo Wilson urges Miriam to join the Lycurgans (Dorothy Richardson's name for the Fabians). She decides to enter the society in spite of her awareness of the nature of Wilson's own commitment: he understood the theory behind it "so well that he must already be believing in something else." Accustomed to the rapidity of the movement of his mind, she feels sure that once she has dedicated herself passionately to socialism he will have sloughed it off. Just as Dorothy Richardson allowed Miriam to perceive the headlong motion of Wilson, so G. K. Chesterton saw Wells, about whom he once remarked: "You can lie awake at night and listen to him grow."

In *Pilgrimage*, Dorothy Richardson's heroine not only finds it difficult to keep intellectual pace with Hypo Wilson, but also faces the problem of the bewildering variety of his moods. He may be kind and admiring one moment, ironic and oblivious the next. Fully attentive to nothing except science, he is capable of reducing even that to absurdity in the playtime of evening—offering, for example, as his "answer to the claims of the feminists, the idea of having infants scooped out early on, and artificially reared." But in the mornings, as preparation for work, he listens to the Beethoven Seventh, liking its last movement best

"because it did so much with a theme that was almost nothing."
He expresses a fondness for Bach, too, and then adds with delight
that he finds women in his music. Mocking, caustic, merciless,
and yet capable of sudden acts of sympathy or generosity, Wilson
in *Pilgrimage* is portrayed by Dorothy Richardson as Wells later
confirmed himself to be in the autobiography she proofread for
him and saw through the press while he was visiting Russia.

During the '20s and '30s, while Wells the world-figure talked
with Lenin and Stalin in the Kremlin, with successive presidents
in the White House, and with Freud and Jung too, Dorothy
Richardson went on portraying Wells the man in the process of
becoming that world figure. She also tried to suggest the manner
in which Wells dispersed himself in his own fiction. In several of
the novels he wrote between 1909 and 1920 can be found a
successful, ubiquitous author named Wilkins. He embodies
certain aspects of the Wells who had already won fame, a
measure of notoriety, and was on the way to earning a
considerable fortune. Wilkins appears as a Fabian in *Ann Veronica*
(1909), published the year after Wells resigned from the society
(and generating a storm because of its heroine's unabashed
inquisitiveness about sex). In *The Passionate Friends* (1913) and *The
Wife of Sir Isaac Harman* (1914), Wilkins is a novelist who calls
himself (in the latter book) an "ideologist" and—like all literary
men—a "rotter": "we *aren't* trustworthy, we aren't consistent.
Our virtues are our vices. *My* life . . . won't bear examination. . . ." In *Boon* (1915), he is one of George Boon's verbal
sparring-partners, and in *Mr. Britling Sees It Through* (1916) a
voluble English patriot such as Wells became during both world
wars. So that when Dorothy Richardson's heroine, attending a
Lycurgan-Fabian Christmas dance, notices "Wilkins the author,
gesticulating greetings," fiction collides with fiction to produce a
reverberating fact—the presence of Wells in *Pilgrimage*, as in
reality and his own novels, in more than one disguise.

But as clearly as Dorothy Richardson saw Wells behind his
various appearances, she could not entirely escape the narrowing
effects of her personal vision. In her portrait of the man, there are
traces of her tendency to dwell—with a certain satisfaction—on
what she considered were his deficiencies as a human being.
Often, however, by means of humor or conscious exaggeration,
she mitigated the tendency. Though she knew only too well the

shortcomings of "H.G.," she was equally aware of his formidable gifts. As a result, both his failings and his talents are dramatized in the emotional relationship she designed between her heroine and Hypo Wilson.

They are physically attracted to one another. When Wilson admits he likes having her about, and Miriam confesses there is a "way" in which he obliterates other men for her, he suggests they "explore each other and stop nowhere." For Wilson, such a proposal raises only the problem of execution—to be solved with effort and time. For Miriam, however, there are difficulties inherent in the situation and compounded by Wilson's proce-dure. It offends her. He conducts his systematic pursuit of her with "flourishes of *deliberate* guilt and *deliberate* daring," even with attempts at "coercion." The effect is to drive her off, to intensify her resistance of the man who—despite his attractiveness—seems empty beneath his "marvellous phrases and pictures." Most of all, she rebels against his "planned" declarations of love. "Behind the sacred words," she feels, is "nothing for her individually, for any one individually." Hypo's primary interest, she tells herself, lies in what a person might become for *him*. He does not care about what she is: "of the essential individual [he] knew, and wanted to know, nothing at all." To her own concern with "being" or essence, he scornfully applies the label of "turnip-emotion."

Her quarrel with Wilson is substantially the same as Arnold Bennett's and Joseph Conrad's with Wells. Bennett, although more mildly critical of Wells than of others, occasionally reared his head and barked back at his pontifical friend. In one of his outbursts, he accused Wells of not being "interested in individual humanity," and predicted he would get "worse and worse, more and more specialised, more and more scornful." In spite of the fact that Bennett's words on this occasion had been prompted in some measure by his personal experience of Wells's scorn and condescension, his remarks were justified. Joseph Conrad, for one, would have agreed with him, as his well-known comment indicates: "The difference between us, Wells, is fundamental. You don't care for humanity but think they are to be improved. I love humanity but know they are not!"

Dorothy Richardson had the advantage over Bennett and Conrad of a more extensive as well as private range of

observation. She was able, therefore, to penetrate behind the wall
of facts and postulates Wells had built, where the draper's
apprentice, the science student, and the adventurous young
writer still existed. Thus in *Pilgrimage* she gives to Miriam the
lingering certainty that "far away within himself" there is a
Hypo Wilson he perpetually denies, "who believed all she
wanted him to believe and knew all she wanted him to know."
She provides grounds for that conviction by endowing Miriam
with the memory of an afternoon early in her friendship with
Wilson. They were sitting together in his study beside a glowing
fireplace. She had been speaking with animation; he had been so
unusually silent she had forgotten he was there. Then after a few
words from him she could never remember, she had been
shocked by the "unspeakably gentle touch" of his hand on her
head. She would feel that "light pressure" all her life and the
way his palm had rested in her fire-warmed hair. It had brought
a moment of still and deep love between them, and kept alive for
a long time her faith that "in spite of his ceaseless denials he saw
and felt a reality that thought could neither touch nor express."

Dorothy Richardson made it quite clear in her comments
about Wells that she did not concur with certain judgments of
him expressed by other people (such as Hugh Walpole, who
feared that "malevolence" lurked in Wells). Thus she permits her
heroine to cling to the hope of meeting again the Hypo Wilson
she had briefly glimpsed on that afternoon, and to continue to
allow him to approach her. But he in turn continues to plunge
forward impatiently, insisting upon achievement, concentrating
his immense vitality on obtaining full possession of Miriam. Like
Wells, who claimed that when he wanted "to get somewhere" he
walked "as straight" as he could because it was "the best way to
get there," Wilson always chooses the shortest possible route. His
method is disconcerting, to say the least, especially when
combined with a "ceaselessly presiding" mind. Wilson never
rests. He manipulates, works at Miriam, demands to be followed.
If a woman refused to be his "disciple," to "play up and make
him believe [she] was following," then she became for him
"merely pleasant or unpleasant biological material." To consent
to play his game is to be be rewarded with his charming society,
his sympathetic understanding, his unlimited intelligence—and
"the little creak in his voice" that appeared only when he was

about to be entertained. The "temptation" is difficult to resist. Wells himself had rarely been resisted. In Dorothy Richardson's view, however, he wanted a woman close enough to him so that she might "burn incense," but not so near as to get in his way.

In accordance with her view of Wells, she allows Miriam to see at last that to sustain the self-denying role Wilson required of a woman would be as difficult as resisting the temptations of his charm. The extent to which Miriam's subjugation might be carried is brought fully home to her on the night Wilson enters her bedroom and stands "over her like a short doctor: flattering, warning, trying to edit her mind." Indignantly she sends him away, but they both know he will return, as he does the following night, and not be repulsed again. Miriam has decided to accept the challenge Wilson is unaware of having made—the challenge that a physical relationship with him would present to the "feminine consciousness" which he steadfastly refuses to recognize as of a "different order" from his own. She feels it necessary at times to be silent, to share a feeling without words, to be known without being labeled. But rarely does Hypo Wilson venture to communicate in other than the "language of 'honest fact'." Time and again he insists that nothing would ever get itself done if all people were to explore the "depths of personalities." Yet there is in him an "unused, self-repudiated personality" that showed itself to her in a few unguarded instants. Otherwise it remains concealed beneath the public Wilson totally engaged in "mankind's immediate affairs," in stating them so clearly and vitally that it often seems even to Miriam, "under the spell of his writing," that "all human activities should cease while he said his say." But the spell is invariably broken by an intensive and exploited "text-book term," and the truth reaffirmed—that Wilson's theories do not for her "encompass reality." Nor did Wells's, for Dorothy Richardson. She thought that all he had succeeded in doing was to "split things up," and then found himself unable to "get them back" no matter how hard he tried.

Dorothy Richardson makes Wilson's theories just as fragmentary to Miriam. They are insufficient, in her estimation, largely because they attempt to understand everything, to leave nothing unexplained, and at the same time ignore the individual who remains unconvinced precisely because he is ignored. In more than mere jest, she denounces Wilson as a "scientific socialist" as well as an opponent of freedom; he counters by labeling her a "Tory-Anarchist." Wearying finally of her efforts to argue that the "scientific metaphors" abounding in his work are a form of tyranny (an accusation Dorothy Richardson often hurled at Wells), she bids goodbye to him one evening as they walk through the streets of London. The path she has come to realize as the essential one for her to take—the same route Dorothy Richardson followed—will lead her in an entirely different direction and ultimately, in the last volume of *Pilgrimage*, to the writing of an autobiographical "stream of consciousness" novel in which Hypo Wilson will act out the double meanings of his name.

Wilson says to her, when she is on the point of leaving London, "Don't chuck your friends, Miriam. . . . You'll still hold me up, be interested in my work? . . . A friend *advises* . . ." Whether or not H. G. Wells ever uttered these words to Dorothy Richardson, their friendship did endure, she supported him in his single unsuccessful stand for Parliament, and she continued to proof-read—for the pay he knew she needed—several of his books. His best writing never lost its power to evoke in her the kind of furiously critical thought that had been the battleground of their relationship. As she herself put it, she could always "sharpen her teeth" on "first-class Wells." But she remained convinced that he had enclosed himself in his narrowing mind and bolted the door. He refused to admit alternatives to his own views, she felt, and locked out entire areas of human experience. To him, the spiritual and psychic needs of the individual were merely trifles. She wondered, too, if he had not "sacrificed his genius to his talent." His cleverness and quickness had indeed conspired to keep him on the surface of life, where he was content to remain so long as the surface was also the "top." For there it was Wells had always wanted to be.

He had made his upward climb with a will whose force Dorothy Richardson could measure. On a small scale, it led him to rage in determined disbelief when she wrote to him once to ask his help for a dying, impoverished friend of theirs, and then to fall silent for weeks when she angrily reported the death. On a larger scale, it turned him into the self-named enfant terrible for life, who became more threatening and strident the less the world listened to him. It drove him to argue defiantly that salvation was possible only if humanity came under the guardianship of a scientifically trained "elite"; to attack individual members of the British aristocracy; and to ridicule the "stuffy little corner of art" in which he claimed he had been sensible enough not to hide. He was the arch-journalist, he proudly declared, as well as the thinking and thus political animal he thought all men ought to be; and he took great pleasure in the necessary consequence of these—a "subversive career," in his own words, which he enjoyed leading to the very end. In the last piece he published before his death, in the summer of 1946, he succeeded in shocking London once more by demanding that the monarchy be abolished.

On a grand scale, however, Wells had driven himself from the tiny shop in Bromley to the palatial home in Regent's Park, London, which he refused to leave during the war even though its windows were shattered several times. After the war, when word of his impending death was relayed to Dorothy Richardson, she wrote to a friend that for those who knew him the disappearance of Wells would have the effect of a "major landslide." In her comment lies the quintessence of the man who was indeed a natural force, though he had harnessed his energy to serve in greatest measure the demands of his will.

Dorothy Richardson's remark points to an important unifying source of Wells's strength. A more direct approach than hers was that of the psychologist Jung, in his essay titled "The Relations between the Ego and the Unconscious" (translated into English in 1928). One of Wells's novels, *Christina Alberta's Father* (published in 1925), impressed Jung as an example of "inner transformation," of the way in which "subtle inner processes [can] invade the conscious mind with . . . suggestive force." Jung was referring to the experience of a mild, passive, dreamy-eyed little man Wells created in this novel. The man (whose royal names, Albert Edward, are combined with Preemby) comes to believe himself a reincarnation of Sargon, ancient King of Sumeria. He tries to resume what he also believes to be his rightful role in the government of the world. When his skeptical, rational daughter attempts to convince him that he has merely dreamed his new (or old) identity, the stolid answer he gives is indeed Jungian: "How could I dream of things I had never seen nor heard of before?" He has experienced a great need to transform his pale slavery of a life into an imperious reign; and he has tapped what Jung called "the collective unconscious."

His daughter doubts him; he slips away from her in search of the subjects he is certain he will find (for he has already seen, walking through the streets, other reincarnated Sumerians); and, before she can prevent it, he is certified a lunatic and committed to an institution. In the course of trying to free him, Christina Alberta finds her actual father, who never suspected that the girl he had been involved with in his youth had borne his child. He is now a wealthy, handsome, strong, intelligent psychiatrist—the antithesis of the poor little man she had always believed to be her father. They take possession of each other so hungrily that, in a comic reversal of the father-daughter pattern and a burlesque of "transference" (Christina Alberta, more than he, becomes the object of dependent love), the psychiatrist must break away eventually by marrying. Before he does so, he manages to reassure the rescued and badly shaken "lunatic" that merely as Mr. Preemby he shares in the common inheritance of all men, that "when [he] called [himself] Sargon, King of Kings, and proposed to rule all the world [he] was *symbolizing*. Of course, everybody is really Sargon, King of Kings, and everybody ought to take hold of all the world and save it and rule it."

Even while spoofing psychiatry and psychology, Wells predicted the dominant role these would play in modern life, and anticipated Jungian theories not yet fully worked out. His story demonstrates the most characteristic elements in Wells: his cleverness, his alert responsiveness to the contemporary world, and his gift of "prophecy." Not least, it expresses his belief that "everybody ought to take hold of all the world and save it and rule it." Indeed if others are reluctant, he will do it alone—both the saving and the ruling. The boy born in Atlas House spent the greater part of his eighty-year life trying to convince the world that it ought to lean upon H. G. Wells.

Unlike the troubled Sargon of his novel, who died of pneumonia before he could begin to practice what the psychiatrist had preached (and even if he had lived, would have continued to inspire love rather than confidence), Wells made himself heard. The little man of *Christina Alberta's Father* is a recurring type, however, in much of Wells's fiction; it was as if the novelist were compelled to explore what he himself would have become had he resignedly accepted his original destiny. He had been a small, weak, ill-fed youth; he had craved strength and authority. The middle-aged creator of Mr. Preemby understandably caught the attention of Jung as illustrating "inner transformation."

Poor Mr. Preemby had realized, under examination, that by continuing to insist he was Sargon he would ensure his commitment, but in giving his real name he would also be giving up the identity he wanted so desperately. If Wells in turn had not maintained the many-sided public self he had worked to create, he would have been left with none. If, furthermore, he had not insisted that life was but a "peculiar throb in matter," he would not have known *what* it was. And he needed profoundly to know. He needed as well to trust in the beneficent and responsible power of the mind over hate and cruelty and greed—even to the extent of willing that it be so, but also taunting the world with its failure to make it so.

Wells's preoccupation with the world and his own relationship to it has led to the contemporary charge that he can "offer nothing" where "the needs of the unique and innermost self are concerned." Admittedly, he refused to focus on the individual consciousness, and transformed nearly all personal feeling into articulate Wellsian monologues or dialogues that hammered out a social or political point of view. Thus it may be tempting to deny him any deep insight into the private human situation. Even Dorothy Richardson was so tempted in her portrayal of Hypo Wilson. But she knew better, having seen Wells without the armor he did not always wear in his novels, either. The impulse to "confess" which she found throughout his work stemmed from a genuine awareness of the problems of the self and a curiously mixed desire both to solve and to deride them.

Yet Dorothy Richardson would have nodded in vigorous agreement with another of Wells's critical friends, Henry James, who broke with him in 1915 after Wells had published his unfeeling and defensive attack in *Boon* on the elder novelist's devotion to art. James—who had recognized Wells's gifts and encouraged their development in the direction of form and discipline—commented once on the strangeness of the "coexistence" in Wells of "so much life with (so to speak) so little living."

Dorothy Richardson might not have defined life in exactly the
same way as James, but she had assessed Wells similarly by
describing the Wilson of *Pilgrimage* as "two people"—one who
delighted in compelling himself toward quick accomplishment
and success, the other "a man seeming uncreated, without any
existence worth the name." That is to say, in order to triumph
where Mr. Preemby had failed, Wells tried to conceal the self
that Dorothy Richardson, in the person of Miriam, sought to
uncover. Wells seemed faintly conscious, nonetheless, of this self
which had been molded during his boyhood in Atlas House. He
apologized in his autobiography for speaking as if he alone were
carrying the burdens of the world, and tried to counter such an
impression by constantly referring to himself as a type or
"sample" rather than an individual. He also attempted to deal
there with the accusations leveled at him by Bennett, Conrad,
James, and Dorothy Richardson. He admitted that more than
ever before he was taking an interest in individuality, and offered
as explanation that earlier he had not been "adult" and
"philosophical" enough to study character exhaustively. "So
much of [his] life," he went on to point out, had been a
"prolonged and enlarged adolescence, an encounter with the
world in general, that the observation of character began to play
a leading part in it only in [his] later years. It was necessary for
[him] to reconstruct the frame in which individual lives as a
whole had to be lived, before [he] could concentrate upon any of
the individual problems of fitting them into this frame."

Four years after the autobiography, in 1938, Wells published a
story titled "The Brothers." The "frame" seems once more to be
the world and its large grave problems, but is really again, as in
Christina Alberta's Father, a psychological one. The undeclared war
being waged in the tale is the background for the meeting of twin
brothers unknown to each other. They are not only on opposite
sides of the ideological fence but also the leaders of their
respective forces. When one of them is captured by the army of
the other, and they are brought face to face, the psychological
impact of their identical appearance is very great. As they talk,
however, it becomes clear they are alike in more subtle ways.
Despite the ideological difference between them, they have
almost a single nature, and they are both engaged in the war for
similar personal reasons. The captor-brother is deeply shaken by

this discovery of a second self. He even toys with the notion of taking the place of his twin—ostensibly as a brilliant maneuver to win the war but in reality because he has come to *be* the head of the opposing force. Argued out of his plan by his advisors, who think the resemblance of the two men merely accidental and who urge that the captured leader be executed, he contrives the escape of his brother. It is foiled by the most devoted of his aides, who catches sight of the fleeing prisoner and shoots him. But he kills his enraged leader as well, in the latter's unsuccessful struggle to prevent the shot from being fired. Although the personal relationship had become more important and valuable than either an ideology or a lifetime of ambition, the consequence of such a reversal is death.

In other words, Wells had made his uneasy, half-conscious, impossible choice long ago—to leap over the abyss of the self in order to satisfy its imperious demands. In his old age—with the world he had addressed all his life, and tried to dominate, on the brink of disaster once again—he seems to have felt the need to justify his decision in the most elementary terms he could imagine. The way he had chosen meant life; the way he had rejected would have brought death. In the process of trying to find comfort, or perhaps even absolution, Wells had become so intrigued by the response a human being might make to a sudden and profound relation that, nearly fifteen years after *Christina Alberta's Father*, he projected another psychological conflict. Since the days of the earlier novel, Wells was apparently of two minds about Freud and Jung and the twentieth-century exploration of the psyche (although he made use of Jungian terms in his autobiography). To be divided, however, was tantamount for Wells to failure and extinction. Hence the little man deep within him and open to self-doubt—the soulful Preemby whom everybody loved, as Dorothy Richardson said of H. G. the artist, and nobody "took seriously"—had to be suppressed. To Wells's intents and purposes, he had been. But the eye of the novelist—his own and Dorothy Richardson's—found him out.

Chronology of Important Dates

1866   H. G. Wells born at Bromley, Kent (21 September).

1881   Enters Midhurst Grammar School.

1881–83   Drapers' apprentice, Southsea.

1883–84   Pupil-teacher at Midhurst Grammar School

1884–87   Student at Normal School (later Royal College) of Science, Kensington.

1891   Marries Isabel Wells.

1894   Elopes with Amy Catherine (Jane) Robbins.

1895   *The Time Machine.*
        Marries Catherine.

1898   *The War of the Worlds.*

1901   *The First Men in the Moon.*
        George Philip Wells born.

1903   Frank Richard Wells born.
        Joins Fabian Society.

1905   *A Modern Utopia.*
        Kipps.

1908   Abandons Fabians after many disagreements.

1909   *Tono-Bungay.*

1910   *The History of Mr. Polly.*

1914   First World War.
        Anthony West (son) born.

1915   Quarrel with Henry James.

1920   *The Outline of History.*
        Meets Lenin.

1927   Death of Catherine Wells.

1933   *The Shape of Things to Come.*

1934   *Experiment in Autobiography.*
          Meets Stalin and Roosevelt.

1936   *Things to Come* (film).

1939   Second World War.

1945   *Mind at the End of Its Tether.*

1946   Death of H. G. Wells (13 August).

Notes on the Editor and Contributors

BERNARD BERGONZI is Professor of English at the University of Warwick. He is the author of, among other books, *The Early H. G. Wells* (1961), *The Situation of the Novel* (1970), and *The Turn of a Century: Essays on Victorian and Modern English Literature* (1973).

ANTHONY WEST, son of H. G. Wells and Rebecca West, is the author of *On a Dark Night* (1949), *Another Kind* (1951), *The Trend is Up* (1960), and several other novels.

ROBERT P. WEEKS is Professor of English at the University of Michigan and editor of *Commonwealth vs. Sacco and Vanzetti* (1958) and *Hemingway* (1962).

V. S. PRITCHETT, distinguished English man of letters, is the author of *Dead Man Leading* (1937), *The Living Novel* (1946), *Mr. Beluncle* (1951), and many other books of fiction and criticism. He was knighted in 1975.

ROBERT M. PHILMUS teaches at Loyola College, Concordia University, Montreal. He has edited, with David Y. Hughes, *H. G. Wells: Early Writings in Science and Science Fiction* (1974).

PATRICK PARRINDER is lecturer in English at the University of Reading. He is author of *H. G. Wells* (1970) and editor of *H. G. Wells: The Critical Heritage* (1972).

WILLIAM BELLAMY, author of *The Novels of Wells, Bennett and Galsworthy 1890–1910* (1971), has taught at La Trobe University in Australia and now practices as a solicitor in Cambridge, England.

DAVID LODGE, Reader in English at the University of Birmingham, is the author of *Language of Fiction* (1966), *The Novelist at the Crossroads* (1971) and several novels, the most recent of which is *Changing Places* (1975).

LUCILLE HERBERT is Associate Professor of English at York University, Toronto.

GLORIA GLIKIN FROMM is Associate Professor of English in the Chicago Circle of the University of Illinois.

Selected Bibliography

The best collected edition of H. G. Wells's work is the Atlantic Edition in twenty-eight volumes (London, 1924–27), containing approved texts and a preface to each volume by the author.

Life and Letters

Vincent Brome. *H. G. Wells: A Biography*. London, 1952.

Lovat Dickson. *H. G. Wells: His Turbulent Life and Times*. London, 1969.

Leon Edel and Gordon N. Ray, eds. *Henry James and H. G. Wells* (letters). London, 1958.

Royal A. Gettmann, ed. *George Gissing and H. G. Wells* (letters). London, 1961.

Norman and Jeanne Mackenzie. *The Time Traveller: The Life of H. G. Wells*. London, 1973.

Gordon N. Ray. *H. G. Wells and Rebecca West*. London, 1974.

H. G. Wells. *Experiment in Autobiography*. London, 1934.

Geoffrey West. *H. G. Wells: A Sketch for a Portrait*. London, 1930.

Harris Wilson, ed. *Arnold Bennett and H. G. Wells* (letters). London, 1960.

Criticism

Bernard Bergonzi. "The Publication of *The Time Machine* 1894–95." *Review of English Studies*, n.s. XI (1960).

———. "The Correspondence of Gissing and Wells," "*Tono-Bungay*," and "Wells, Fiction and Politics," in *The Turn of a Century*. London and New York, 1973.

Christopher Caudwell. "H. G. Wells: A Study in Utopianism," in *Studies in a Dying Culture*. London, 1938.

G. K. Chesterton. "Mr. H. G. Wells and the Giants," in *Heretics*. London, 1905.

Richard Ellmann. "Two Faces of Edward," in *Edwardians and Late Victorians*. Edited by Richard Ellmann. New York, 1960.

Richard Gerber. *Utopian Fantasy*. London, 1955.

Mark R. Hillegas. *The Future as Nightmare: H. G. Wells and the Anti-Utopians*. New York, 1967.

Samuel Hynes. *The Edwardian Turn of Mind*. Princeton, 1968.

————. "H. G. and G. B. S.," in *Edwardian Occasions*. London, 1972.

Christopher Isherwood. "H. G. Wells," in *Exhumations*. New York and London, 1966.

J. Kagarlitski. *The Life and Thought of H. G. Wells* (Translated by M. Budberg).London, 1966.

D. H. Lawrence. "*The World of William Clissold* by H. G. Wells," in *Selected Literary Criticism*. Edited by Anthony Beal. London, 1956.

David Lodge. "Assessing H. G. Wells" and "Utopia and Criticism: the Radical Longing for Paradise," in *The Novelist at the Crossroads*. London and Cornell, 1971.

A. L. Morton. *The English Utopia*. London, 1952.

Kenneth B. Newall. "The Structure of H. G. Wells's *Tono-Bungay*," in *English Fiction in Transition*. IV (1961).

————."*Kipps* and the Masterman Episode." *PMLA*. 86 (1971).

Norman Nicholson. *H. G. Wells*. London, 1950.

George Orwell. "Wells, Hitler and the World State," in *Collected Essays, Journalism and Letters*, Vol. 2. London, 1968.

Patrick Parrinder, ed. *H. G. Wells: The Critical Heritage*. London, 1972.

————. "Imagining the Future: Zamyatin and Wells." *Science Fiction Studies*. I (Spring, 1973).

Ingvald Raknem. *H. G. Wells and His Critics*. London, 1962.

Gordon N. Ray. "H. G. Wells Tries to be a Novelist," in *Edwardians and Late Victorians*. Edited by Richard Ellmann. New York, 1960.

W. Warren Wagar. *H. G. Wells and the World State*. New Haven, 1961.

Harris Wilson. "The Death of Masterman: A Repressed Episode in H. G. Wells's *Kipps*." *PMLA*. 86 (1971).